NATURE
WALKS
in & around
PORTLAND

NATURE
WALKS
in & around
PORTLAND

All-Season Exploring in Parks, Forests, and Wetlands

Second Edition
Previously published as *A Pedestrian's Portland*

Karen and Terry Whitehill

THE
MOUNTAINEERS

Published by
The Mountaineers
1001 SW Klickitat Way, Suite 201
Seattle, WA 98134

Previously published in 1989 as *A Pedestrian's Portland*
Second edition, 1998

Published simultaneously in Great Britain by Cordee, 3a DeMontfort Street, Leicester, England, LE1 7HD

Printed in Canada

Edited by Paula Thurman
Maps by Debbie Newell
All photographs by Karen and Terry Whitehill
Cover design by Ani Rucki
Book design by Alice C. Merrill
Book layout by Margarite Hargrave
Cover photograph: *Azalea and dogwood tree in full bloom beside Crystal Springs Lake at Crystal Springs Rhododendron Gardens, Portland, Oregon* ©Rick Schafer
    Inset: *The evening vista from the heights of Powell Butte Nature Park* ©Whitehill
Frontispiece: *Downtown Portland as seen through a window in the greenery along the Terwilliger Boulevard*

Library of Congress Cataloging-in-Publication Data
Whitehill, Karen, 1957–
    Nature walks in & around Portland / Karen and Terry Whitehill.—
2nd ed.
        p.   cm.
    Rev. ed. of: A pedestrian's Portland. c1989.
    ISBN 0-89886-563-8
    1. Walking—Oregon—Portland—Guidebooks. 2. Natural history—
Oregon—Portland—Guidebooks. 3. Portland (Or.)—Guidebooks.
I. Whitehill, Terry, 1954–   . II. Whitehill, Karen, 1957–
Pedestrian's Portland. III. Title.
GV199.42.072P678 1998
917.95'490443—dc21   97-51847
                                                          CIP

*For our children, Sierra, Rocky, and Aliya—
may you always find joy in exploring, and may you always
delight in the places these trails take you.*

Contents

Introduction / 11

Why Nature Walks? / 11
Why Walk at All? / 11
Why Here? / 12
When to Walk / 13
Where to Walk In and Around Portland / 15
A Note About Safety / 16

Central Area / 19
  1. Terwilliger Boulevard (Duniway Park to Capitol Highway) / 19
  2. Himes Park to Willamette Park / 23
  3. Willamette Park and Willamette Greenway Trail / 27
  4. Marquam Nature Park to Council Crest / 31
  5. Washington Park Rose Garden to Pittock Mansion / 36
  6. Washington Park Rose Garden to World Forestry Center / 42

North Portland and Clark County / 47
  7. University of Portland / 47
  8. Smith and Bybee Lakes Natural Area / 51
  9. Kelley Point Park / 55
  10. Burntbridge Creek Greenway / 59
  11. Salmon Creek Greenway / 63
  12. Lacamas Park / 66

Northeast Portland / 72
  13. The Grotto / 72
  14. Rose City Golf Course / 77
  15. Glendoveer Fitness Course / 82

Southeast Portland and Environs / 88
  16. Laurelhurst Park / 88
  17. Mount Tabor Park / 92
  18. Powell Butte Nature Park / 98

Mount Hood makes a stunning backdrop to a walk along Terwilliger Boulevard.

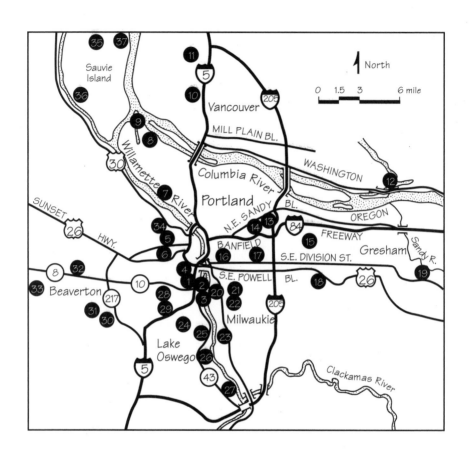

19. Oxbow Regional Park / 103
20. Oaks Bottom Wildlife Refuge / 107
21. Reed College and Crystal Springs Rhododendron Garden / 113
22. Tideman-Johnson Park / 119
23. Elk Rock Island / 122

Southwest Portland and Environs / 128
24. Marshall Park / 128
25. Tryon Creek State Park / 131
26. George Rogers Park / 136
27. Mary S. Young State Park / 139
28. Gabriel Park / 144
29. Woods Memorial Park / 148
30. Fanno Farm House and Greenway Park / 152
31. Hyland Forest Park / 156
32. Tualatin Hills Nature Park / 160
33. Jackson Bottom Wetlands / 164

Northwest Portland / 170
34. Lower Macleay Park / 170
35. Sauvie Island—Oak Island / 174
36. Sauvie Island—Virginia Lake / 178
37. Sauvie Island—Warrior Rock / 181

Index / 187

Introduction

Why Nature Walks?

When this book was first published in 1989, it was titled *A Pedestrian's Portland—40 Walks in Portland Parks and Neighborhoods*. It was aimed at the casual walker, and its focus was mostly on urban walking within city parks and neighborhoods. With this second edition, we've chosen a new title— *Nature Walks In and Around Portland*. And we have a new focus—nature.

There are still some walks that traverse urban parklands described in this edition. We've kept many of our favorite city hikes intact, simply double-checking details and rewriting with a closer eye on wildlife, birds, trees, and flowers.

But we've also added some new hikes to the mix, spotlighting some long-established parks that are a little farther away from Portland's center and adding some recently established natural areas that are part of the region's ongoing commitment to preservation of our wilderness heritage.

So if you live in Clark County, Washington, there are more hikes in your neighborhood listed in this book. And if you're part of Beaverton's outward sprawl, there are some new areas for you to look at, too. Or if you're simply interested in getting to know the natural areas of Portland and its surroundings a little bit better, you'll find help with your quest in the following pages.

Why Walk at All?

In this era of rollerblades and mountain bikes, of windsurfing and snowboarding, why does anyone walk at all anymore? Perhaps to escape the "tyranny of gear." If you've ever wished that life was a little simpler, or if you've ever dreamt that all the contraptions and complexities that clutter your existence would suddenly disappear, you'll find great potential here. Walking is simplicity.

Don't feel like you have to go shopping for a pair of $100 hiking boots before you set out on the trails this book describes. Don't think you have to pull on an expensive rain jacket before you brave the Pacific Northwest's "liquid sunshine." Don't stop to strap on a portable radio or stick a set of headphones in your ears.

Simply go for a walk. Just listen. Pause and look. There's life all around you here—in the forest, in the wetlands, in the little parks where birds and

Lower Macleay Park offers a forested escape from Portland's pavement.

animals still live, where wildflowers burst into blossom every spring, and where trees continue to reach their limbs toward the sky.

And while you're walking, tune out the city and tune in to the earth. The wonders of nature are still here—behind the high-rise buildings, on the edge of the pavement, whispering beneath the autos' roar.

Savor the caress of the sun on your shoulders. Inhale the freshness of a light spring rain. Or close your eyes and listen to the birds chattering in the trees.

That's what walking has to offer. Peace. Simplicity. A slice of sanity in a world of motorized chaos. A chance to see things at a pace that enhances observation and enjoyment. A chance to forget the race to the next adventure or the crawl to the next traffic light.

Why Here?

This book's purpose is to tell you where to walk close to home, to give you ideas for Saturday strolls or after-dinner jaunts, to make you aware of interesting parks and natural areas—not in faraway destinations on Mount Hood or the Pacific Coast, but in places just outside your own back door, spots right here in and around Portland, Oregon.

Portland is blessed with a multitude of lovely parks, roughly 180 of them. They encompass 11 percent of the city's land area, and they range in size from tiny Mill Ends Park (listed in the Guinness Book of World Records as the smallest city park in the United States) to sprawling Forest Park (weighing in at more than 5,000 acres).

Portland's commitment to urban greenery goes back almost as far as the city does. The tree-lined corridor that forms the downtown park blocks was set aside in the mid-1800s, and Portland's growing 40-Mile Loop is part of a city parks plan formulated way back in 1904. The 40-Mile Loop was originally conceived of as a 40-mile trail encircling the city. Today, loop planners estimate the popular urban trail system will connect more than 30 city parks and measure at least 140 miles upon its completion sometime near the end of this century.

Portland is an attractive city, a city with more than its share of greenery and, mercifully, little urban blight. It's a city that's worth getting to know. The urban areas around Portland are blessed with a plenitude of parks, as well. Clark County has more than a dozen great hike destinations. Beaverton to the west, Gresham to the east, Lake Oswego and Oregon City, too—if you want to walk, there are opportunities everywhere!

Think of that little marsh or forest you've always driven by but never stopped to explore. Ever wondered if herons visit the pond or fish live in the stream? Maybe you've pondered what kind of trees grow beside the paths or what sort of wildflowers bloom there in the spring. Do you think it might be fun to find out where that little trail goes? Perhaps you'll find the answer in this book.

When to Walk

What's the best time of day to walk in the Portland area? Ask a dozen walkers, and you'll get a dozen answers. Some people like to walk first thing in the morning, before breakfast, a shower, or work. Others can't even lace their shoes without a cup of coffee, and some wouldn't dream of physical exertion before the clock strikes noon. The main thing to remember is this—pick a time that's good for you, and go!

Inquisitive squirrels patrol the pathways of the Glendoveer Fitness Course.

If you'll be walking alone, be sure to take personal safety into account when choosing a hiking time. Metropolitan trails are generally busiest on weekends and afternoons. Be careful when visiting an isolated area or when hiking during non-peak hours.

Use caution when choosing your walks, too. Find a companion when you plan to explore more isolated trails, especially routes that take you deep into the forest. Our often-slick trails provide great potential for twisted ankles and falls. It's nice to have someone along if an accident does happen.

If you must hike alone in an isolated area, be sure to let someone know where you'll be. Carry extra clothing if the weather is unsettled, and take along a flashlight if it's getting late. Read through the walk description before you go so that you'll know what to expect in terms of terrain and distance.

The Pacific Northwest's mild climate makes year-round walking both possible and desirable. There are very few days in the year when Portland's low-elevation trails are covered with snow (although there are scores of days

Birdwatching is a delight at Smith and Bybee Lakes Natural Area.

when mud puddles rule). And our region's well-earned reputation for a lot of rain makes it easy to select appropriate attire on cloudy days. When in doubt, assume it's going to pour.

Bring along an umbrella, a rain hat, an overcoat and/or waterproof shoes—depending on the degree of dryness you want to maintain. Or plan to take a long, hot shower after your hike; dress warmly, and don't worry about a little drizzle on your back.

All the trails described in this book are negotiable in tennis shoes; however, muddy pathways can be slippery. If the weather is damp, wear shoes with lots of tread.

If you're hiking with children, be sure to talk about trail safety with them before you begin. Stress the importance of staying together, and talk about appropriate behavior in the event of separation. Have your child wear a whistle when hiking in forested areas. Be sure to talk about water safety with your children, too—many of the hikes in this volume are along lakes and streams.

Finally, set a good example for your children with your own behavior. Stay on established trails, leave birds and animals undisturbed, and carry out your garbage.

Convenience, climate, caution—work with these variables in deciding when to walk. Then go for it!

Where to Walk In and Around Portland

This book will give you many ideas for nearby places to explore, providing you with new insights on walks you thought you were familiar with and introducing you to some places you never knew were there.

The walks are grouped by area, and numbered consecutively, with the lowest numbers corresponding to hikes closest to Portland's central core. Next are those in north Portland and Clark County. Following in a clockwise direction around the city, the highest numbers are located in the southwest and northwest quadrants of the greater urban area. Refer to the overall city map in the front of the book if you're looking for a walk in a particular area or trying to pinpoint one of the descriptions.

Each walk write-up gives information on distance, estimated time required, highlights, terrain, and best time of year to go. A detailed discussion of plants and trees is included in each walk description, too. If you find that the botanical information piques your appetite for wildflower labeling, birdwatching, or tree identification, consider carrying a field guide along on your forest explorations.

Information on access and parking, degree of difficulty and accessibility to strollers and wheelchairs, historical tidbits, comments on vistas and picnic spots—all of these are woven into the text so that your walks will be even more enjoyable.

So now that you're ready—read, walk, and discover *Nature Walks In and Around Portland.*

A Note About Safety

Safety is an important concern in all outdoor activities. No guidebook can alert you to every hazard or anticipate the limitations of every reader. Therefore, the descriptions of roads, trails, routes, and natural features in this book are not representations that a particular place or excursion will be safe for your party. When you follow any of the routes described in this book, you assume responsibility for your own safety. Under normal conditions, such excursions require the usual attention to traffic, road and trail conditions, weather, terrain, the capabilities of your party, and other factors. Because many of the lands in this book are subject to development and/or change of ownership, conditions may have changed since this book was written that make your use of some of these routes unwise. Always check for current conditions, obey posted private property signs, and avoid confrontations with property owners or managers. Keeping informed on current conditions and exercising common sense are the keys to a safe, enjoyable outing.

—*The Mountaineers*

Snowberry bushes glow in the shadows left by a winter sun.

Central Area

◆ 1 ◆
Terwilliger Boulevard
(Duniway Park to Capitol Highway)

Distance: 2¾ miles (one way)
Estimated time required: 1 hour and 15 minutes
Highlights: Wonderful views of the Willamette, downtown Portland, and
  Cascade peaks
Terrain: Steady uphill grade on paved path; fine for strollers and wheelchairs
Best time to go: Great all year, but a clear day makes the walk truly grand

Background Terwilliger Boulevard has its origins in a 1904 park plan laid
out by an urban planning whiz kid named John Olmsted. This farsighted
Boston landscape architect was called to Portland to oversee the layout of
the 1905 Lewis and Clark Exposition. He was responsible for the design of
Portland's Laurelhurst Park as well (see Walk 16). Olmsted envisioned construction of a scenic boulevard along the side of Marquam Hill—a boulevard
that would give car-happy Portlanders a cruise with a view.

The land for Terwilliger Boulevard was donated on the condition that
the scenic thoroughfare not be used for commercial traffic, and work on the
road began in 1911. Although Terwilliger Boulevard has become a busy commuter route to downtown Portland since its early days as a pleasure drive into
the countryside, the city of Portland has made efforts to adhere to the
Terwilliger tradition, including the construction of a parallel bikeway along
the boulevard. In recent years, that bikeway has become the favorite haunt
of joggers and walkers, and cyclists have been moved onto bicycle lanes beside the path. Terwilliger's foot travelers often number in the hundreds on
sunny weekend afternoons.

One trip along the boulevard and it's easy to see why Terwilliger is so
popular with walkers. The Willamette's journey through downtown Portland
is played out at a pedestrian's feet. On a clear day, the views to the east and
north are tantalizing. Mount Hood, Mount St. Helens, and Mount Adams
are often visible. Occasionally, a snow-capped Mount Rainier puts in an appearance. Even on a cloudy day, the hillside beside the pathway is a green
wilderness of assorted conifers and deciduous trees.

Douglas firs stand tall beside the Terwilliger Boulevard walking path.

Although the near-constant hum of traffic is often irritating on this busy boulevard, the songs of birds are audible as well. And the even pavement of the pedestrian path makes this a perfect year-round hike. It's ideal for strollers and wheelchairs, too.

We've written this hike for the most scenic (and popular) section of Terwilliger Boulevard—from Duniway Park to Southwest Capitol Highway. However, it is possible to continue with the Terwilliger walking route to Southwest Barbur Boulevard. In addition, the walk in Himes Park (Walk 2) can be used as a connecting route between the Terwilliger jaunt and a stroll through Willamette Park (Walk 3).

Getting There Reach Duniway Park and the start of the Terwilliger bikeway via Tri-Met Bus 8 (on Southwest Terwilliger Boulevard) or Buses 1, 5, 12, 45, or 55 (on Southwest Barbur Boulevard). If you're driving, there's limited parking on the east side of Duniway Park, beside the jogging oval. You can get to the lot by driving south on Fifth Avenue from downtown Portland. Follow signs for Southwest Barbur Boulevard, and turn right into the lot as you drive along the edge of Duniway Park. Otherwise, plug a meter on a nearby street, or drive a short distance up Terwilliger Boulevard and leave your car in one of the many scenic pulloffs beside the road.

Duniway Park is named for Abigail Scott Duniway, one of Portland's founding mothers. Duniway was founder and editor of a weekly newspaper from 1871 to 1887. She supported women's rights and was a local leader in the national women's suffrage movement. In 1912, Duniway became the first legal woman voter in Multnomah County.

Getting Around From the parking area beside the Duniway track, walk northwest toward Terwilliger Boulevard, crossing the running oval and gaining an asphalt path ascending toward the road. A stone restroom building will be on your right. Swing to the left, and climb steeply on the asphalt path to parallel Terwilliger Boulevard.

Join the walking path shortly afterward, and continue climbing beside Terwilliger. As you look to the left, you'll see the tree-covered slopes of Marquam Hill. The tan-colored Oregon Health Sciences University Hospital sits astride a lofty saddle straight ahead. Walk beside the crinkly white trunks of handsome European white birches and gain the lighted intersection of Terwilliger and Southwest Sam Jackson Park Road.

Swing left with Terwilliger as you pass a lovely lilac garden painted half a dozen shades of purple in the spring. The scent of the blossoms is overwhelming in late April. Continue steadily uphill, passing a mountain ash tree that's heavy with orange berries in early fall. You'll be delighted by the variety of trees along this walk, and you'll see evidence of careful planting in evenly spaced bigleaf maples and strategically placed cherry trees.

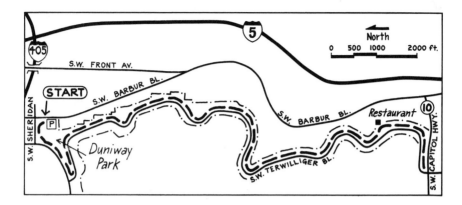

Climb beside tall Port Orford cedars as you continue east. When the walkway curves to the right along the hillside, you'll get your first good view of Portland. Don't linger too long, as there are several impressive vistas still ahead. Gaze down on the span of the Marquam Bridge as you walk south along the hill.

You'll share your way with a lot of runners on this hike, especially in the lower reaches of the route. In recent years, however, walkers have begun to hold their own in the numbers count. The path is lined with sturdy bigleaf maples as you continue to ascend. Not long after the 1-km signpost, watch for the large horsechestnut tree along the path. It's covered with blossoms in early May.

The grade levels out as you reach the turnoff for the dental school and eye clinics. Directly ahead on the ridgetop, you'll see the Veterans' Hospital towering above the city. Stay with the main route as a secondary path descends the hillside to the left, pass one of the many scenic parking pulloffs along the way, and begin to climb more steadily again.

Several old Oregon white oak trees shade the path as you continue up. Walk past the intersection of Southwest Condor Avenue and Terwilliger. A long set of stairs climbs the hillside to the right, leading to the Veterans' Hospital. And tall black cottonwoods tower above, sweetening each breath you take with their aroma.

Come abreast of another parking pulloff. You'll see one of the stations of the Terwilliger exercise course to the left of the bikeway. It's guarded by a group of tall Douglas firs. The forest is green with sword and bracken ferns. Vine maples and huckleberry bushes huddle in the shade, and the delicate white blossoms of Siberian lettuce dot the dark ground like twinkling stars.

Reach the turnoff for the Veterans' Hospital after about 1¼ miles. Continue on to the intersection of Southwest Lowell and Terwilliger, and savor a stretch of downhill walking as you press on.

The trees thin out a bit as you pass above a grassy lawn. Gaze across the roofs for a view of the eastern reaches of the city. The tree-covered island in the middle of the Willamette is Ross Island, home of one of Portland's great blue heron rookeries. Watch for the stately Douglas fir in the second grassy area you pass. From here, you'll have a view south along the river, with the Sellwood Bridge a rainbow for a score of tiny sailboats on a sunny afternoon.

There's a restroom building and an always running drinking fountain at the intersection of Terwilliger and Southwest Hamilton Street. Line up behind a couple of panting joggers to quench your thirst. Your downhill breather is about to end. Walk on beneath tall Douglas firs. Occasionally, their roots disrupt the level surface of the path, shoving the asphalt into cracking wrinkles as they spread. On the hillside to the left, trilliums and yellow stream violets dot the forest floor, and sword ferns duel for the sun. The scent of the trees is a welcome whisper of freshness, tossed back at the belches of passing autos.

Climb steadily through a thick forest of Douglas firs. Red elderberry bushes claim the middle ground, competing with vine maples for the bits of sun the fir trees drop. If you're walking in late August, the sweet smell of Himalayan blackberries will lure you from the asphalt path. Continue your journey up the hill, sporting black fingers and a juice-stained tongue.

Just beyond the second station on the exercise course, watch for the tall, bushy shapes of black cottonwood trees ahead. You'll know the cottonwoods by their shiny leaves and sweet balsam fragrance. Negotiate a short section of the path that's lined with a black metal guardrail, and you're almost to the summit of the hill.

Push on to the Chart House Restaurant. The parking lot in front is open to the public (a good spot to leave a second car, if you're doing a shuttle hike). There's a drinking fountain at the far end. You can walk to the shaded Elk Point Viewpoint on the north end of the restaurant (beside the wooden totem pole). There's a bench here that your weary legs will love.

If you're returning to Duniway Park and your car, this is a good spot to turn for home, as the last stretch to Southwest Capitol Highway is short and unexciting. Tri-Met Bus 8 stops in front of the restaurant, if you're too tired to retrace your steps.

If you're continuing on to Barbur Boulevard or Willamette Park (Walk 3), proceed along the walkway to Capitol Highway, walking steadily downhill for ⅓ mile. Use the crosswalk to negotiate Capitol Highway, and descend along the left edge of Terwilliger Boulevard on the asphalt path. Pass the intersection with Southwest Terwilliger Place, and begin a gentle climb beneath Douglas firs, bigleaf maples, and western red cedars. You'll be walking along the edge of forested George Himes Park.

Wander to the street side of the boulder at the intersection with Nebraska Street, and take a look at the small plaque honoring George Himes, an Oregon historian and pioneer. The intersection with Nebraska marks the start of Walk 2 to Willamette Park, if you're continuing in that direction.

◆ 2 ◆
Himes Park to Willamette Park

Distance: 1 mile (one way)
Estimated time required: 30 minutes
Highlights: Deep forest with many wildflowers
Terrain: Steep descent on primitive trail; no strollers or wheelchairs
Best time to go: A dry day in summer or fall

Background If you're looking for a connecting hike to take you from Southwest Terwilliger Boulevard (Walk 1) to the shore of the Willamette River, the descent through heavily forested Himes Park is an excellent option. The trail is steep and often slick, so wear boots or waffle-soled tennis shoes. If the Portland rain has been falling steadily, you may want to postpone your visit until fairer weather.

Despite the rough hiking, the passage through Himes Park is a pleasant link in Portland's growing trail network. The trail offers a wide variety of wildflowers and native shrubs, and it's shaded by tall conifers. In addition, the Himes Park trail is now an official part of Portland's 40-Mile Loop. As such, it should receive more attention (and perhaps some gravel for the muddy spots) in future years.

For now, however, the trail through Himes Park is primitive and often

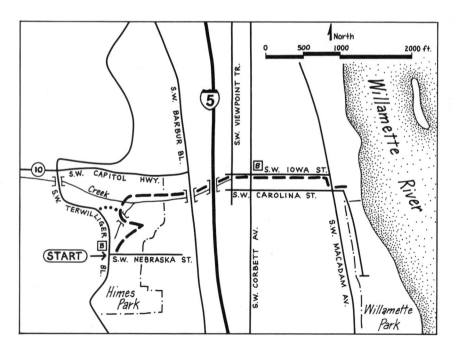

Trilliums sing the joys of spring in Himes Park.

underused. The urban forest serves as a play area for neighborhood children, but you'll often have the byways to yourself as you wander down the hill from Terwilliger Boulevard. If you're looking for a longer hike, you can connect this walk with Walk 3 (Willamette Park) to mix a forest jaunt with a stroll along the river.

Himes Park was named for George H. Himes in 1935. Himes was an Oregon pioneer and historian, born in 1844. He began his duties as secretary of the Oregon Pioneer Association in 1866, and he also served as curator and field secretary of the Oregon Historical Society, beginning in 1898.

Getting There Reach the start of the walk at the intersection of Southwest Nebraska Street and Southwest Terwilliger Boulevard (about ⅓ mile south of Southwest Capitol Highway). There is ample parking just off Terwilliger Boulevard. If you're arriving by bus, Tri-Met Bus 8 runs along Terwilliger. You can come on foot by combining this hike with Walk 1.

Getting Around Begin your walk at the waist-high boulder that marks the intersection of Southwest Terwilliger and Nebraska. Pause on the Terwilliger side of the boulder, and take a look at the bronze plaque honoring George H. Himes. From the boulder, veer left off Nebraska Street to gain a steep footpath taking off into the forest.

A lofty roof of Douglas fir branches will close in above you as you dive downhill on the needle-carpeted path. You'll lose the sound of Terwilliger's traffic within minutes as you continue straight on the main pathway, scrambling steadily down the slope. Inhale deeply, and you'll know you've left the city. The scent of ferns and trees sweetens every breath, and bird songs will trickle through the branches as you walk.

Sword ferns and vine maples line the trail all year long. And Oregon grape and red elderberry bushes compete for space among sun-starved red huckleberries. Wildflowers are abundant in April, May, and June. Watch for the white petals of trilliums if you're visiting early in the season.

Later on, the trilliums are joined by yellow stream violets and the thin white spires of vanilla leaf. In late April and early May, you'll see the odd-shaped blossoms of fringe cups, too. These cream-colored or pale pink flowers cling to long, hairy stalks. The plant's small green leaves cluster near the ground, as if avoiding competition with the tiny blossoms.

Stay on the main trail as you descend, watching your footing carefully. Cars grumbling on Southwest Capitol Highway will be an unwelcome companion as you continue. The trail makes a sharp switchback to the left, and you'll pass a large laurel bush on the right soon afterward. Cross a small stream on a dilapidated wooden bridge. The air is delightfully cool in this little nook, and lady ferns and maidenhair ferns wriggle their toes in the damp soil.

Thimbleberry bushes crowd the trail as you walk on. If you're walking in May or June, watch for the delicate white blossoms of northern inside-out flowers dangling from upright stems. Siberian lettuce is abundant, too, sprinkling the ground with a host of small pinkish-white flowers. You'll probably spot the tiny blossoms of false mitrewort, as well. The flowers are so small, you almost need a magnifying glass to admire them.

Join a second path descending from Terwilliger, and continue downhill through a particularly muddy stretch of trail. Go slowly here. One false step, and you may ski down to the river!

Sword ferns, lady ferns, and red huckleberry bushes are abundant in this section. The trail widens out and becomes more level as you walk beside a narrow stream shaded by bigleaf maples and red alders. You'll see two busy thoroughfares ahead of you, beyond an avenue of Douglas firs. The first road is Barbur Boulevard, the second is Interstate 5.

Walk beneath elevated Barbur Boulevard. The thought of the rough old timbers that support this lofty overpass may make your stomach flutter the next time you drive over in a car. The road's flying leap across this narrow gully is almost indistinguishable from above, but you'll get a feel for the labor of the road builders as you stand at the bottom, gazing up.

Unkempt tangles of Himalayan blackberries clog the gully as you continue. And thin green points of common horsetail spring straight from the ground beneath them, looking like spears of underfed asparagus. In fact, ancient Romans consumed the young plants in much the same way that we eat asparagus today!

Continue descending on a stair-stepped gravel trail and pass beneath the Interstate-5 overpass. You'll gain a narrow footpath marked with wooden steps and see a residential district just ahead.

Leave the shelter of the forest as you emerge on Southwest Iowa Street. There's a Tri-Met bus stop (Bus 43) one block farther east on Southwest Corbett Avenue. If you're continuing to Willamette Park, hike east on Iowa Street until you reach Macadam Avenue. Go right one block to Southwest Carolina Street. Cross Macadam carefully, then follow Carolina toward the river. Willamette Park will be just to your right (south) along the shore.

Yellow stream violets line the forested trail through Himes Park.

♦ 3 ♦
Willamette Park and Willamette Greenway Trail

Distance: 1¾ miles (one way)
Estimated time required: 1 hour
Highlights: Pleasant riverside walk with views of sailboats and sunbathers
Terrain: Level walk on paved path; great for strollers and wheelchairs
Best time to go: Summer afternoons are action packed but noisy; try a
winter day for quiet

Background Willamette Park is a popular Portland sunning spot on summer
afternoons. Families picnic on the grass. Teen-agers toss Frisbees skyward. And
lotion-basted bodies revolve like roasting sausages on beach towels. If you
haven't seen Willamette Park like this, you haven't seen Willamette Park.

But once you've seen it this way, you'll want to visit it again—sometime
when all the sun-loving Portlanders are back at home. Try this walk on a crisp
fall afternoon, or set out on a winter morning when the December sun smiles
on the west bank of the river. You'll savor the quiet you'll find along the shore.
You'll enjoy the easy walking and the mudless pavement. And you'll love the
views of cottonwoods and ducks and patient fishermen—without the roar of
ski boats or the wail of transistor radios.

Getting There Reach Willamette Park from Southwest Macadam Avenue. If
you're coming from downtown, drive south on Macadam, and watch for signs
to Willamette Park not long after the commercial hubbub of John's Landing. You'll turn left across Macadam to enter the park proper. (A moderate
parking fee is charged in the summer months.) Drive south as far as possible,
and park beside the tennis courts.

If you're arriving by bus, there are half-a-dozen lines that run along Southwest Macadam Avenue. Ask for the stop nearest the turnoff for Southwest
Taylor's Ferry Road (on Southwest Nevada Street). Cross Macadam carefully,
and walk toward the south end of the park. For a longer hike, you can link
this walk with Walk 2, Himes Park, as well.

Getting Around From the west side of the tennis courts, walk south on the
paved entrance road, then gain the asphalt path that skirts along the Macadam Avenue side of the park. You'll have a softball diamond on your left as
you walk toward the southern boundary of the park.

Every visitor to Willamette Park should take this little detour to view one
of the park's oldest and most handsome residents. A 240-year-old oak tree
rules the grass at the far end of the park. Its spreading branches form a lovely
canopy against the sky.

Watch for the small bronze plaque beside the asphalt path as you approach the tree. Placed in 1976, the plaque recognizes the oak as a veteran of the American Revolution in 1776. The tree is 53 inches in diameter at shoulder height and 65 to 70 feet high. Local arborists estimate the tree could easily live another 200 years. You'll find few oaks in Portland that are more beautiful than this old warrior.

Stay on the asphalt path as you loop around the tree, and swing north to walk beside the river. The riverbank is lined with tall black cottonwoods. Inhale deeply, and their strong, sweet fragrance will fill your mind with river memories. The black cottonwood (also known as the "western balsam poplar") is the tallest native western hardwood. Its wood is used for boxes, crates, and pulp.

If you have children along on this outing, you might want to walk in the sand beside the river for awhile. If you'd just as soon avoid distractions, keep to the asphalt path and continue north. Speaking of distractions, directly across the water, you'll see the carnival rides and low buildings of Oaks Amusement Park.

The tree-covered lowlands behind the amusement park form the setting for Walk 20, Oaks Bottom Wildlife Refuge. Sailboats dot the surface of the river on breezy spring and summer afternoons. Ski boats are a noisy addition in July and August. And you'll see fishermen hunched above their lines on dreary days in early spring, dreaming of fresh salmon dinners while their fingers freeze.

Follow the asphalt into the heart of Willamette Park, staying on the riverbank. Keep to the right as the path branches into the parking lot, and stroll past picnic tables as you continue. Look south along the river for a view of the Sellwood Bridge. To the north, the high-rise buildings of downtown Portland scramble skyward in the distance.

There are toilets near the boat ramp (to the left, beside public telephones). Continue along the river, winding through a maze of asphalt paths as you go. Gain the northern boundary of the park and curve toward the railroad tracks on the asphalt path. You'll walk past a parking area for the Willamette Sailing Club. Head for the railroad-crossing sign at the far end.

A small blue sign on a wooden post marks the Willamette Greenway Trail. As recently as the 1960s, a four-lane freeway ruled the west shore of the Willamette River through downtown Portland. There was little opportunity for the city's residents to linger on the river's banks. But Oregon Governor Tom McCall and Portland Mayor Terry Shrunk shared a vision of a friendlier Willamette, and that vision became the Willamette Greenway, a ribbon of green that winds through Eugene, Corvallis, and Portland to Kelley Point Park (Walk 9) and the confluence of the Willamette and Columbia.

You'll be exploring a section of this greenway as you continue. Pass to the right of the post and veer sharply to the right to stay on the pedestrian

The Willamette Greenway Trail provides walkers with access to the Willamette shore.

path. You'll regain the riverside as you walk between the water and a ¾-mile stretch of tidy condominiums. This section of the trail is popular with joggers, rollerbladers, and cyclists, as well.

The cottonwood-cluttered island in the middle of the river is Ross Island, home of one of Portland's great blue heron rookeries. The great blue heron is the official bird of the city of Portland. Keep an eye on the treetops as you walk, and you'll probably spot one or two of these ungainly creatures flapping off to feed. Mallards and gulls skim the Willamette's surface all year long. And eels, river otters, beavers, and enormous sturgeon call this ribbon of water home. Take your time as you press on. Who knows what you might discover?

Keep to the lower asphalt trail as secondary branches shoot off into the housing development. Exchange manicured lawns and carefully trimmed shrubs for cottonwoods and Himalayan blackberries as you near the northern reaches of the first cluster of condominiums. The elevated tracks of the periodically revived Portland-to-Lake-Oswego trolley will be on your left as you continue.

Scattered mudflats along the shoreline will be dotted with tiny spotted sandpipers if the water level is low. If you're walking on a clear day, you should be able to see the snow-cloaked tip of Mount Hood across the river to the east. The peak plays peek-a-boo as the asphalt walkway winds through gentle ups and downs.

Nod to yet another bevy of well-padded rollerbladers as you enter another stretch of condominiums, keeping to the riverbank. You'll see the broad span of the Ross Island Bridge to the north as you walk. The Willamette Greenway Trail will dump you unceremoniously in the parking lot of a riverside restaurant. Beat off late-afternoon munchies, and regain the walkway at the far end of the lot. Scotch broom, Himalayan blackberries, and thistles line the bank as you continue.

Wind past more office buildings, a second restaurant, then more office buildings. The official Greenway Trail ends at the northern edge of the River Forum office building. From here, you can retrace your steps to regain your starting point.

If you're in the market for more walking, it is possible to continue on

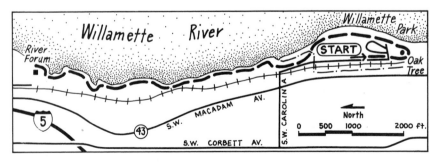

foot all the way to RiverPlace. You'll add about 1⅓ miles to your one-way walk and you'll have to endure a bit of the Willamette's industrial scenery along the way. But the route really isn't unpleasant, and the cafes at RiverPlace make a wonderful destination for a hungry hiker.

To continue, gain an asphalt path beside the railroad tracks as you leave the River Forum office building. Then follow Southwest Moody Avenue toward downtown Portland. There's almost no traffic on Moody on weekend days, and it's sporadic during working hours. You'll have plenty of room along the shoulder. Stay with the flow of walkers, cyclists, joggers, and rollerbladers to find your way to RiverPlace and those munchies you've been waiting for.

◆ 4 ◆
Marquam Nature Park to Council Crest

Distance: 3½ miles (round trip)
Estimated time required: 2 hours
Highlights: Lovely forest walking, a spectacular view from Council Crest
Terrain: Steep climb on an often muddy trail; no wheelchairs or strollers
Best time to go: Super hike on a crystal-clear day; autumn leaves are fabulous

Background The Marquam Nature Trail is yet another example of Portlanders' love for Portland's parks. Through the dedicated efforts of a group called Friends of Marquam Nature Trail, this forested pathway was constructed between Southwest Sam Jackson Park Road and the summit of Portland's highest hill—Council Crest. The Marquam Nature Trail is a lovely link in the growing network of pedestrian paths that forms the city's 40-Mile Loop. This hike can be combined with other paths to take the energetic walker north to Pittock Mansion and beyond, or south and east to the Willamette River and southeast Portland.

The Marquam Nature Trail is outstanding on two counts. One, it begins in the heart of the city, yet it has a wilderness feel to it that few hikes in Portland can match. And, two, it climbs to the 1,070-foot summit of Council Crest to yield a wonderful view of the city in every direction. This is a strenuous hike with an altitude gain of 900 feet, so be sure to do some preliminary walking before you take it on. The trail is rough, and it's often muddy and slick. We recommend that you wear boots or waffle-soled tennis shoes.

There's a drinking fountain atop Council Crest, but you may want to carry extra liquid for the climb. No matter what condition you're in, it'll definitely have you panting. If you want to make the excursion really special, pack a picnic lunch along—but be sure to save it for the top. There are restroom facilities on Council Crest at the base of the radio tower.

A trio of young hikers examines the vegetation beside the Marquam Nature Trail.

Getting There To reach the trailhead at Marquam Nature Park, drive west on Southwest Sam Jackson Park Road about ¼ mile from its junction with Southwest Terwilliger Boulevard. Turn right onto Southwest Marquam Court just after you pass two large water towers (on the right). You'll see a sign for the Marquam Nature Shelter as you pull in. There are about a dozen parking slots in the small lot beside the nature shelter.

If you're arriving by public transit, take Tri-Met Bus 8 to the intersection of Southwest Terwilliger and Sam Jackson Park Road, then walk the ¼ mile to the nature shelter. Be sure to pause at the shelter before you begin your hike. It offers a good map of the trail, as well as several exhibits. You can gather interesting tidbits about the history and vegetation of Council Crest and of Marquam Hill, the lower, hospital-topped mound Portlanders call "Pill Hill."

Getting Around From the nature shelter, take the small paved road heading up the hill. (There's an old roadbed/trail just past it on the left—this hooks in to your route farther up and provides access to the Marquam Hill Trail.) On the right, a cutoff trail beckons toward Southwest Broadway Drive. This will be your return route.

The asphalt road soon becomes a narrow footpath. Continue climbing steadily, and leave the city behind as you enter a thick forest of deciduous trees. Sword ferns and vine maples cover the steep bank to the left of the trail. Negotiate a small set of wooden stairs and continue along the hillside above Marquam Gulch, climbing past Douglas firs, red alders, and bigleaf maples.

As you distance yourself from the city, you'll lose the sound of the traffic on Terwilliger Boulevard and begin hearing the songs of birds instead. A small stream runs its course down Marquam Gulch, and the murmur of its passage will accompany your footsteps.

Trilliums are abundant on the hillside in early spring. Watch for their bright white faces among the ferns. Another wildflower you'll see along the trail in April, May, and June is a small yellow flower known as the stream violet. The stream violet has a five-petaled yellow flower, and its lower three petals are etched with thin maroon lines. Fringe cups are another common wildflower in Marquam Nature Park. They'll be joined by the tiny white blossoms of Siberian lettuce in May and June.

Walk this trail in the winter or early spring, before the trees regain their leaves, and the afternoon sun will be a pleasant companion as you climb, filtering through the branches to warm your face. Wait until August or September to walk, and you might lose the sun, but you should be able to pluck some fruit from the salmonberry and red huckleberry bushes sprinkled along the trail.

Continue climbing steadily. The steep bank to the left is tangled with lovely maidenhair ferns. Occasionally, small streams cross the trail, leaving muddy footprints in their wake. You'll feel like you've walked into a refrigerator as you enter the cool air that surrounds the springs. And you'll be delighted by the blossoms of northern inside-out flowers and false Solomon's seal in spring.

After about ⅖ mile, make a sharp bend to the left to follow a switchback up the hillside. Shortly afterward, you'll reach a marked junction. Take the branch to the right and press on toward Council Crest. Hike through a series of snaking curves as the trail zigs and zags up the hillside. Watch for the bright red berries of the female English holly trees along the way. Red elderberry bushes add their crimson fruit in June. And the red berries of false Solomon's seal bob above the trail in August.

The terrain levels out gradually as you near the crest of the first ridge. You'll see the shapes of houses among the trees and hear the "civilized" clamor of lawnmowers and automobiles trickling down the hill.

Climb steeply up a series of short switchbacks, and keep left at the junction with the trail from Broadway Drive (this is your return route).

Arrive at Southwest Sherwood Drive, cross carefully, and regain the trail on the other side. Continue on level terrain, staying with the main trail as you skirt below several large homes. You may encounter a few bicyclists on this section of the trail. They're invariably riding down the hill, and they're often riding fast. Be prepared to scramble out of the way.

Descend gently to cross a small stream, keeping to the left as the trail branches. Not far beyond the stream, look for a young hemlock tree on the left side of the trail. It's growing out of the decaying wood of a massive old-growth stump. Climb once more, and watch for stream violets and trilliums along the way. Sword ferns, holly, vine maples, and tall old Douglas firs add their presence to the forest atmosphere. You'll be breathing hard by the time the trail levels off again. Remember, the views from Council Crest are still ahead (and, unfortunately, still above).

Ascend steeply to reach Southwest Fairmount Boulevard. This road is busier than Sherwood Drive, so cross with extreme caution. Keep an eye out for cyclists, as this loop around Council Crest is a very popular route. Continue on the well-marked Marquam Hill Trail, taking a much-deserved breather as the trail winds gently along the hillside. Lady ferns, sword ferns, and Oregon grape bushes line the way.

A wealth of wildflowers enriches this stretch as well. Between the months of April and June, you'll be able to see false Solomon's seal, Siberian lettuce, Smith's fairybell, northern inside-out flowers, fringe cups, and wild ginger, to name a few.

Continue on to Southwest Greenway Avenue, the main auto route to Council Crest. It's very busy on sunny weekend afternoons. Cross carefully and regain the trail for the last steep ascent to the summit. You'll see the Council Crest radio towers piercing the sky above as you climb.

Some say Council Crest got its name from the Indian conferences that took place on the hilltop before white settlers moved in. The breezy heights must have made an impressive setting for the tribal councils in those days. Today the hilltop is a favorite with Portland's picnickers.

If you're fortunate enough to time your walk so that it coincides with a bit of cloudless weather, you'll have a spectacular view of several Cascade peaks from the top. Mount Rainier, Mount St. Helens, Mount Adams, Mount Hood, and even Mount Jefferson are all within sighting distance from Council Crest. Scramble up to the small brick enclosure on the grassy hilltop. The arrows and names engraved within will help you identify the distant mountains.

Closer in, you'll be able to spot the green mounds of Rocky Butte, Mount Tabor (Walk 17), and Mount Scott in east Portland. To the south, the buildings of the Oregon Health Sciences University crown Marquam Hill. Beaverton stretches toward the horizon in the west. And to the north, the buildings of downtown Portland are dwarfed by distance, looking like a child's construction set.

If you have the time and inclination, choose a soft patch of grass and settle down to enjoy your favorite section of the view. About this time, you'll be glad for the picnic lunch you trundled up the hill—despite all your grumbling on the steepest pitches. And you can smile smugly as you watch the Crest's steady flow of visitors stumble numbly from their cars to absorb the vista. They may enjoy the hilltop just as much as you, but think of all the sights they missed on the way up!

In the early 1900s, a streetcar puffed up the hill to the summit of Council Crest. The hilltop held a popular amusement park then, complete with roller coaster, a land-locked riverboat, and dance hall. You may wish you had

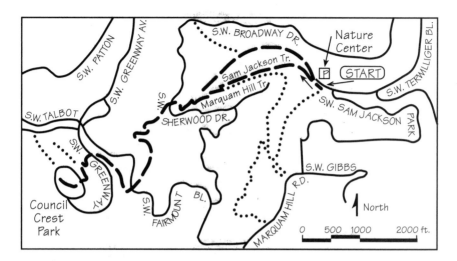

a streetcar to carry you back down as you begin to contemplate your return hike to the Marquam Nature Park. Actually, Tri-Met Bus 51 does run along Greenway Avenue on its way to downtown Portland, so public transport is an option.

On the other hand, if you're still full of energy after slogging up the hill (or if your picnic lunch revived you just enough to make you feel like a world-beater today), you can hook up with the Marquam Trail toward the World Forestry Center from Council Crest. This will take you down and across the Sunset Highway and onward to the Washington Park Zoo (and a tie-in with Walk 6). Refer to a good map and give it a try, if you're in the mood.

If you're walking back to your starting point, return to the Terwilliger Trail and retrace your steps down the hillside, crossing Greenway Avenue, Fairmount Boulevard, and Sherwood Drive. You can backtrack all the way to the nature shelter if you wish. Otherwise, add some new terrain to your return route by backtracking to the marked junction just below Sherwood Drive. Go left here to finish your descent along the "sunny side" of Marquam Gulch.

Walk gently downhill as you skirt along the hillside, making your way toward Southwest Terwilliger Boulevard. If you're walking in the spring, watch for starflowers, vanilla leaf, fringe cups, and Siberian lettuce beside the trail. A special treat awaits the wildflower fan in June. That's when the showy blossoms of the crimson columbine unfold among the greenery. Scattered bursts of sunshine and the melody of bird songs add to the pleasure of your journey down the hill.

Bypass the side trail leading up toward Broadway Drive, and let your weary legs slip into neutral as the slope leads you steadily downward toward the nature shelter and your starting point. You'll be there before you know it, ready to dive back into the city with a reluctant sigh.

◆ 5 ◆
Washington Park Rose Garden
to Pittock Mansion

Distance: 4 miles (round trip)
Estimated time required: 2 hours
Highlights: On a clear day, the view from Pittock Mansion is one of
   Portland's finest
Terrain: Rough trails and many hills; no wheelchairs or strollers
Best time to go: April for trilliums, May for roses, summer for sun

Background Both this walk and Walk 6, Washington Park Rose Garden to
World Forestry Center, begin at Portland's International Rose Test Garden
in Washington Park. Located on a hill overlooking downtown Portland, the
Willamette River, and the city's eastern quadrant, Washington Park is truly
one of Portland's greatest treasures. This park combines with Macleay and
Forest Parks and Hoyt Arboretum to form one of the largest enclaves of
parkland within city limits anywhere in the United States.

   Although the park proper, with its tennis courts, picnic areas, and summer concerts, is loved and utilized by scores of Portlanders, the trails criss-
crossing the forested hills that stretch toward the north and west are often
silent and deserted—and always wonderful to explore.

   If you have time, take a stroll through the International Rose Test Garden before beginning your walk. Founded in 1917, it's the oldest rose test
garden in the United States, with more than 300 varieties of roses growing
in its well-kept beds. The roses are particularly beautiful in late May and early
June, coinciding with Portland's Rose Festival. Savor the view of the city from
the top level of the amphitheater, then turn toward the tennis courts and the
upper parking lot.

Getting There Reach the Rose Garden via Tri-Met Bus 63, which runs along
Southwest Salmon Street and climbs Southwest Park Place to Washington
Park (and on to Washington Park Zoo). Or gain access to the park by car
from West Burnside Street. Turn left onto Southwest Tichner Drive, and
follow the signs for the Japanese Garden. There is ample parking just above
the Rose Garden and the tennis courts.

Getting Around Walk to a sign for the Japanese Garden opposite the tennis
courts, and continue up a paved entrance road. Go left to walk beneath a
handsome ornamental gateway, and begin climbing on a serpentine gravel
path, negotiating several switchbacks as you ascend. (On the rare occasions
when the Japanese Garden is closed to visitors, the gateway may be closed, as

Picnickers and hikers enjoy the landscaped grounds of Portland's Pittock Mansion.

well. You can access the trailhead by continuing up with the paved entrance road instead.)

If you're walking in the spring, you'll be delighted by an array of wild-flowers as you climb. False Solomon's seal bobs on long, thin stems beside the trail, its white blossoms dripping with sweet perfume. Fringe cups pour their tiny cup-shaped blossoms into the pool of flowers, and white-petaled thimbleberries join in.

Emerge onto a paved area, and pass the entry booth to the Japanese Garden as you follow the curving road to the right. Watch for an unpaved path veering off to the left soon afterward. It's marked with a small, nearly overgrown sign that says "To Wildwood Trail." Climb steeply on the trail through a series of switchbacks.

You'll notice lady ferns and dark green English ivy crouching at your feet. Wild roses add their delicate pink blossoms in the summer months. Climb steadily and leave the city behind, with only the sound of your breathing and the songs of the birds for company. Keep to the left at the first junction, fol-lowing the sign for the Wildwood Trail as you walk through a forest of Dou-glas firs, western hemlocks, and bigleaf maples. Oregon grape bushes and sword ferns compete for the ground around the tree trunks.

You'll be breathing hard by the time you arrive at an overlook spot above the Japanese Garden. If you have children along, be sure to keep them safely away from the edge. The dropoff is very steep. Pause for a lofty look at the beautifully landscaped grounds of the Japanese Garden. Not only will you enjoy the view but it's a good excuse to stop and catch your breath!

Continue climbing, staying on the main trail and ignoring the smaller paths veering off to the left and right. Reach a junction with the Wildwood Trail. You'll go right to continue toward Pittock Mansion. The walking becomes more level as you skirt along the hillside on the Wildwood Trail. Forest Park's Wildwood Trail is the major thoroughfare through Washington Park, Hoyt Arboretum, and Macleay Park. It measures a winding 25+ miles from end to end, and it's a major part of the overall plan for Portland's 40-Mile Loop.

Descend slightly after a few minutes and cross a small creek gully surrounded by red elderberry bushes, thimbleberries, and common horsetail. It's interesting that common horsetail is one of the most widespread plants in the world. Many gardeners detest it, however, and some call it by its other name, "devil guts."

You'll climb into Hoyt Arboretum as you leave the water. Your progress may slow a bit here, not because the hills are steeper but because many of the trees in the arboretum have small plaques on their trunks giving their common and scientific names. You'll probably want to pause to read them as you go along.

Things open up a bit in the arboretum, and the grassy hillsides gather a lot of light. Watch for the purple blossoms of common vetch tucked in among the tufts of grass. And look for fringe cups and yellow stream violets turning their bright faces toward the sun. Reach a sign for the Winter Garden (to the left), and continue to the right on the Wildwood Trail. (This junction is the linking spot with the following hike, Walk 6, Washington Park Rose Garden to World Forestry Center.)

Cross two paved roads—Southwest Cascade Drive and Southwest Upper Cascade Drive—and continue upward on the Wildwood Trail. Look to the right as you skirt the hillside to catch a view (if it's clear) of the Columbia River, the Sam Jackson Bridge, and Washington's Mount Adams. Climb gradually and pass a side trail joining from the right, then arrive at another junction (Oak Trail) and stay with the Wildwood Trail to the right.

Just before you reach Southwest Fairview Boulevard, the embankment beside the trail is tangled with Himalayan blackberry bushes. These non-native invaders thrive where the absence of trees allows plenty of sun to fall on them. Cross Fairview Boulevard, taking advantage of the two-way stop sign to claim your pedestrian right of way. Tri-Met Bus 63 stops here between the Washington Park Rose Garden and the Washington Park Zoo.

Dive right onto the Wildwood Trail once again. Descend through a handsome growth of Ponderosa pines. There's a sunny picnic area with several tables on the left. Enter a denser forest where light and shade leave lovely patterns on the trees. You'll begin to hear murmurs from the traffic on Burnside Street as you continue down the hill. If you're walking in the spring, you'll have a host of wildflowers to brighten your way.

False Solomon's seal bobs beside the trail on long, leafy stems, making the forest fragrant in May, and Pacific waterleaf adds its shaggy purple blossoms to the springtime color scheme. Sword ferns and salal cover the forest floor with green, and tall trees toss their shadows to the ground. Reach a signpost at a junction and stay on the Wildwood Trail, continuing straight.

Giant sequoias and California redwoods line the next part of the trail. These are some of the most handsome trees you'll see all day. Marvel at their massive, red-hued trunks as you walk. Stay with the Wildwood Trail as it zigzags down through the forest, then turn right onto a small wooden bridge to cross a tiny creek. Pause on the bridge to inhale deeply the damp, pine-scented air.

Leave the area of the arboretum with labeled trees, and climb through growths of western red cedar and Douglas fir. In May, northern inside-out flowers hang like tiny ballerinas on thin stems, and false mitrewort dances on delicate green threads in June. Thimbleberry, red elderberry, and red huckleberry bushes crowd in among the ever-present ferns.

Arrive at another junction and angle right with the Wildwood Trail, noting a small board that says "Pittock Mansion 1 Mi." on the signpost. Gain more level terrain, then descend slightly as you approach Burnside Street. The roar of Burnside's traffic is particularly unpleasant after the silence of the forest, and the road can be extremely busy from 4 to 6 P.M., when commuter traffic is at its height. Use great caution when crossing, as cars are traveling very rapidly. Scurry across Burnside and regain the steeply ascending Wildwood Trail on the other side. You'll hardly notice the incline in your eagerness to distance yourself from the traffic noise.

Climb steadily on the unpaved trail. Many parts of this walk can be quite muddy in wet weather, and footing will be slick. Watch for small pinkish-white flowers scattered in among the ferns along the trail. These are the blossoms of Siberian lettuce. They're present from April to June. If you walk the path in March or April, you'll see legions of trilliums in their brilliant white Easter outfits. And yellow stream violets and pink-rimmed fringe cups join the wildflower fashion show in May.

Ascend steadily for about ¼ mile, cross a small access road, and continue upward on the trail. As traffic noise grows fainter, you'll begin to hear the voices of the birds again. (Of course, that's assuming that your labored breathing doesn't completely drown them out.) Watch for the occasional massive trunk of an old Douglas fir among the thinner pines and deciduous trees. The smooth bark of the skinny vine maples looks as tender as a baby's bottom, compared with the weathered countenances of the rough-skinned Douglas firs.

The trail emerges on Northwest Pittock Drive, the auto route into the

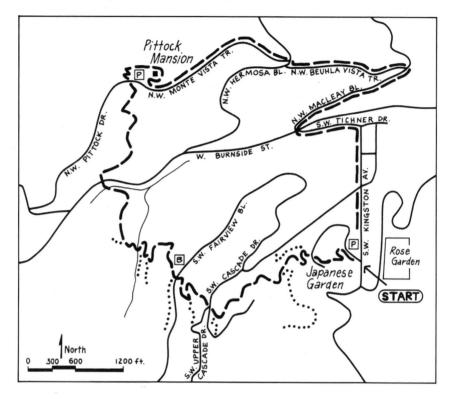

mansion and surrounding park. Cross the road and follow the trail upward, noting the steep banks decorated with purple and white foxglove. Wind through trees for several hundred feet, climbing steadily. You'll see two special plants on this part of your walk. They're both identifiable by their leaves.

Watch for small plants boasting triangular-shaped leaves about 6 inches off the ground. Flip a leaf upside down, and you'll see a pale green arrow pointing down the trail. This is the leaf of the pathfinder plant. Another small plant found along this part of the trail boasts paired, heart-shaped leaves. Rustle under the greenery and search for a small brownish flower lying on the ground. This is the blossom of wild ginger, and it has a scent in keeping with its name. In pioneer days, the stems and roots of wild ginger were used as a substitute for the valuable spice.

Arrive at the upper end of the Pittock Mansion parking lot. From here the Wildwood Trail continues down the opposite side of the ridge toward Macleay Park (see Walk 34, Lower Macleay Park). The large parking area beside the mansion provides a good spot to leave a second car if you want to establish a shuttle and walk only half of this loop. It's used heavily by the many joggers who frequent the trail.

Descend through the parking lot to Pittock Mansion and Pittock Acres Park. You'll pass a small souvenir shop and public restroom on the left. There's a drinking fountain on one end of the building.

Pittock Mansion has been a Portland landmark since 1914, when the initial construction was completed. The mansion was built by Henry Pittock, a wealthy newspaperman, and the fine-looking building is a testimony to his taste for the best building materials the Northwest had to offer. The gray-green walls of the mansion are constructed of Tenino sandstone from Tenino, Washington, and the bright orange-red tile roof makes the mansion a conspicuous landmark, visible from many places in Portland.

The mansion sits atop a ridge 940 feet above sea level, and it rules a 46-acre estate that belongs to the city of Portland. The interior of the mansion is open for visits daily from noon to 4 P.M. (An entry fee is charged.)

Approach the mansion and swing to the left through luxurious grounds, colorful with rhododendrons, azaleas, roses, and petunia-dotted flower beds. Walk out onto the grassy point in front of the mansion, and turn your back on the city to get the most impressive view of Henry Pittock's house. The mansion dominates an emerald lawn that simply begs for picnics. There are tables and benches scattered on the point, or spread your feast on a patch of grass and savor the view as you eat.

On a clear day, several Cascade peaks can be seen from this vantage point. From left to right, look for distant Mount Rainier, flat-topped Mount St. Helens, a glowing white Mount Adams, and Mount Hood, Oregon's highest peak. If visibility is less than ideal, you'll probably be lucky to spot Mount Hood and Mount St. Helens.

The green, city-surrounded mound slightly to the left of the line with Mount Hood is Mount Tabor (Walk 17), and the second mound, farther to the left, is Rocky Butte. The lofty ridge to the south, surmounted by a large radio tower and a pale green water tank, is Council Crest (Walk 4).

After you've feasted on the view and/or a picnic lunch, you'll have a decision to make. You can simply backtrack to your starting point, enjoying a double dose of this wonderful urban forestland. Or you can see some new territory as you pace the pavement, passing million-dollar dwellings clinging to the heights above downtown.

To hike back by the new route, continue south along the paved walkway, descending past banks of giant rhododendrons (magnificent in April) to reach the refurbished Gate Lodge. It's now a tearoom, serving lunch Monday through Saturday. Walk past a chain barrier and turn left onto a paved road to walk below the Gate Lodge.

Leave the environs of Pittock Acres Park as you reach a padlocked gate. Go out through the pedestrian opening on the right. Descend steeply on Northwest Monte Vista Terrace, and sneak million-dollar views through the living-room windows of the homes that line the road. Keep to the right at the first junction, and continue down to Hermosa Boulevard. Cross Hermosa and go left on Northwest Beuhla Vista Terrace. There are no sidewalks on these streets, but traffic is very light.

Descend steeply on Beuhla Vista, passing a junction with Verde Vista. Just after the junction, watch for a large terraced garden on the left. This rose-filled wonderland was once voted the No. 1 Victory Garden in the United States. A landslide destroyed much of the garden during one of Portland's rain-drenched winters a few years ago, but it's still worth a look.

Reach a junction with Rainier Terrace, and continue down Beuhla Vista. Stay on Beuhla Vista past Lomita Terrace. A glance to the right will reveal a fine view of the Washington Park Rose Garden and amphitheater on the hillside to the south.

Beuhla Vista runs into Macleay Boulevard. Turn right on Macleay, and continue your descent. You'll pick up a little more traffic here, but there's a sidewalk on the left side of the road. Descend on Macleay Boulevard to the busy Burnside corridor, and cross cautiously, gaining the paved road (Southwest Tichner Drive) that climbs up the hill on the other side.

Turn right on Kingston Avenue, following signs for the Japanese Garden and the Rose Garden. Climb gently, admiring the impressive mansions along the left side of the road. Enter the Rose Garden parking lot to complete your loop.

◆ **6** ◆
Washington Park Rose Garden to World Forestry Center

Distance: 4 miles (round trip)
Estimated time required: 2 hours
Highlights: Wildflowers are abundant in the spring; the forest is grand all year
Terrain: Unpaved trails and a steady climb; no wheelchairs or strollers
Best time to go: Spring for forest flowers; all year for handsome trees

Background Like Walk 5, Washington Park Rose Garden to Pittock Mansion, this walk begins at Portland's International Rose Test Garden in Washington Park. Turn back to the introductory material for Walk 5 if you'd like some background on Washington Park.

From Washington Park, you'll climb steadily through a lush forest of Douglas firs, western hemlocks, and bigleaf maples to arrive at Portland's World Forestry Center and the Washington Park Zoo. It's an uphill haul to the ridge above the Forestry Center, but the walk back down is pleasant and effortless.

If you'd prefer a shorter hike, you can establish a car shuttle by leaving a vehicle at both ends of the walk. Or you can utilize Tri-Met Bus 63, which runs between the Rose Garden and the Zoo.

If you have the time, plan to take a break at the World Forestry Center when you complete the first half of the walk. It is open from 10 A.M. to 5 P.M., seven days a week. (An admission fee is charged.) You'll find a host of interesting and informative displays inside. Your return walk through the forest will be even more fascinating after your visit.

Getting There Reach the Rose Garden via Tri-Met Bus 63, which runs along Southwest Salmon Street and climbs Southwest Park Place to Washington Park (and on to the Washington Park Zoo). Or gain access to the park by car from West Burnside Street. Turn left onto Southwest Tichner Drive, and follow the signs for the Japanese Garden. There is ample parking just above the Rose Garden and the tennis courts.

Getting Around Walk to a sign for the Japanese Garden opposite the tennis courts, and continue up a paved entrance road. From here, follow the same path used to visit the Pittock Mansion (Walk 5). When you reach a sign for the Winter Garden, however, veer left to continue toward the World Forestry

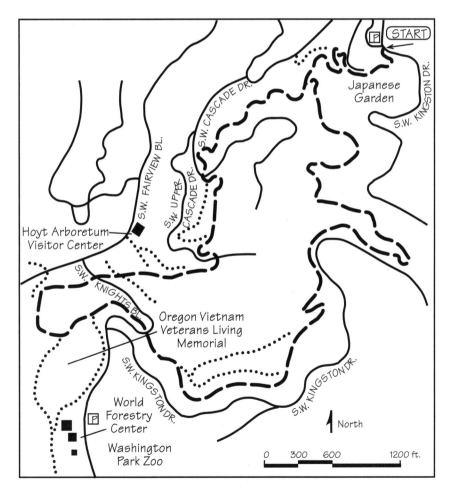

Center. (The route for Pittock Mansion turns off to the right.)

Pass a shaggy western red cedar as you wind uphill on the snaking trail. You'll notice a wide variety of non-native trees as you continue. Many of the arboretum's trees are labeled, so you'll have quick access to information if you're curious about their names. Cross paved Southwest Cascade Drive, and gain the Magnolia Trail by following the signpost on the other side.

Angle left at the next junction, staying with signs for the Magnolia Trail. You'll climb beneath several lovely homes as you continue. Fringe cups and false Solomon's seal brighten the trailsides. Off to the right, watch for a large planting of magnolia trees. Their branches are heavy with blossoms in the early spring.

Keep straight on the Magnolia Trail at the next junction. Pause at a wooden bench where the trail makes a sharp bend to the left, and gaze across the Burnside Corridor. You'll see the red-roofed Pittock Mansion on the opposite ridge. Continue climbing beside a bank sprinkled with delicate wild strawberries. You'll pass between a couple of California bay trees a little farther on. Break one of the stiff leaves between your fingers, and inhale the telltale scent.

Just before you emerge onto Southwest Upper Cascade Drive, watch for white-faced daisies and the enchanting blossoms of crimson columbine beside the trail (blossoming in June). Cross paved Upper Cascade Drive and regain the footpath on the other side.

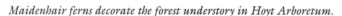

Maidenhair ferns decorate the forest understory in Hoyt Arboretum.

If you're walking in spring, you'll see the bright yellow blossoms of heavy-laden golden chain trees as you continue. Climb to the next junction and continue straight on the Wildwood Trail, passing on the right-hand side of a large water tank.

Stay with the ridgetop Wildwood Trail, and sneak some more looks at Pittock Mansion as you walk. The Cherry Trail will join you from the left as you continue. To the south, you'll have a nice view of Council Crest, Portland's highest hill. (If you're not fed up with climbing, try Walk 4, Marquam Nature Park, for the ascent of Council Crest. It's also possible to reach Council Crest from the World Forestry Center. Refer to a map of Forest Park to find the trail.)

Pause at the marker on the right side of the trail, and peer into the distance to search for the landmarks it calls out. If you would like to pay a quick visit to the arboretum's visitor center, you can continue with the trail past the view area and reach the center soon afterward. It's open daytime hours (as volunteer help allows), seven days a week. You can pick up maps, brochures, books, and information on arboretum tree tours here.

To proceed with your hike toward the Forestry Center, cross the wide trail as you leave the marker, and take a smaller gravel path south between two pines. Descend gently on the Wildwood Trail, admiring a handsome Pacific madrone on the right side of the trail as you walk. Cross paved Southwest Knights Boulevard, and continue on the Wildwood Trail.

If you're walking in April or May, watch for the purple blossoms of tough-leaved irises hiding on the bank as you descend. Wild strawberries add their small white flowers to the color scheme as well. Enter a shaded grove of Douglas firs, and continue straight on the Wildwood Trail as the Hemlock Trail joins in from the right.

You'll be nearing the World Forestry Center and the Oregon Vietnam Veterans Living Memorial as you meander on beneath tall Douglas Firs. If you have the time, visits to both spots are well worthwhile. Catch your breath and contemplate on a bench within the lovely environs of the memorial, or take one of the trails leading to the right to reach the buildings of the Forestry Center. (The Marquam Trail leads on toward Council Crest from here.)

To begin your hike back toward the Washington Park Rose Garden, take the signed Maple Trail off of the Wildwood Trail. (The junction is just above the memorial.) You'll pass a wide variety of non-native trees as you wind along the hillside. Descend gently to cross Knights Boulevard, and continue on the Maple Trail. You'll delight in the brilliantly colored maple leaves if you're walking in the fall. There are more than 100 species in the maple family, and a good number of them are represented here.

Reach another trail junction, and stay right on the Maple Trail. Pass a turnoff for the Hawthorn Trail, and descend gently along the slope. You'll have open hiking for a time, then enter a deeper forest of Douglas firs and western hemlocks. Watch for tough-leaved irises as you walk.

You'll see trilliums in the early months of spring in this part of the woods, and salal lines the pathway with its evergreen foliage all year. The dark berries of the salal bushes are edible (if not particularly tasty). In fact, Pacific Northwest Indians dried the fruit and pounded it into small cakes. Another edible berry you'll see along the trail is that of Oregon's state flower, the Oregon grape. Forest animals are fond of Oregon grape berries, and they can be mashed and cooked to make a tasty jelly. Northwest Indians utilized the bark and wood of the plant to make a yellow dye.

Curve gently uphill, and join the Walnut Trail as you angle to the right. Leave the forest briefly, then turn right onto the Wildwood Trail to dive into the forest once again. This section of the walk is a florist shop of wildflowers in the spring. Watch for stream violets, fringe cups, Siberian lettuce, and false Solomon's seal.

Descend steadily on the wide footpath. You'll come in beside Southwest Kingston Drive as you walk along the lower edge of a grassy picnic area. Regain the forest on the other side. Climb gently in the shade of Douglas firs and bigleaf maples, then continue your descent. You'll have lots of trilliums for company if you're walking here in March or April. Stay on the Wildwood Trail as a footpath joins in from the left, then pass a second footpath merging from a roadside parking area on the right.

Cross a small creek where maidenhair ferns are tangled on the bank, and climb gently to cross another stream. You'll see the landscaped grounds of the Japanese Garden down the steep hillside to the right as you continue. If you're looking for an excuse to catch your breath, stop and count the fat orange carp in the dark pool within the garden's serene enclave.

Stay on the main trail as you curve around the hillside, then make a sharp turn to the left where a dead-end trail shoots off toward the edge of the bluff. You'll reach a junction soon afterward where the Japanese Garden Trail climbs in from the right. Go right to continue your descent toward your starting point.

North Portland and Clark County

University of Portland

Distance: 1½ miles (round trip)
Estimated time required: 30 minutes
Highlights: Pleasant view from bluff above the Willamette; landscaped grounds with wide variety of trees and shrubs
Best time to go: Try a spring weekend to avoid classes and find the best in blossoms
Terrain: Flat walking on paved walks and grass; strollers are okay, wheelchairs must make detours to stay on walkways

Background If you're looking for a pleasant stroll in a parklike setting, try a visit to the University of Portland campus some sunny weekend day. Since its establishment as a Catholic university in 1901, the University of Portland has benefitted from a long succession of skilled gardeners who have lavished the grounds with plenty of loving care. Today, the campus boasts a renowned camellia collection, a rare rhododendron garden, a host of conifers, and countless varieties of flowers.

The land known as "Waud's Bluff" (after pioneer John Waud, who sold the property in 1891) was still mostly farm and pastureland when the university's Brother Ferdinand Moser began to work his charms on it in 1933. Brother Moser's first love was camellias, and he planted more than 65 varieties during his 30 years at the university. Moser added rhododendrons and assorted trees as well.

His work was followed upon by the university's first full-time horticulturist, Ted Deiss. Deiss helped establish a species rhododendron garden on campus. ("Species" rhododendrons are rhododendrons found growing naturally in the wild.) The University of Portland's species garden contains more than 40 different representatives of rhododendrons from as far away as China, Tibet, and the Himalayas.

We've written a suggested walking tour of the campus to help you on your initial visit, but the many intersecting walkways offer a host of other possibilities. If you enjoy your first walk here, plan a return trip at a different time of year. The campus offers a display of flowering plants throughout the seasons.

You can mix in a neighborhood stroll with your campus walk by exploring North Willamette Boulevard in either direction from the university environs. Willamette Boulevard is a popular promenade for the university's neighbors, and you'll be joined by joggers, dog walkers, and strollers as you explore the surrounding neighborhoods.

Getting There You can reach the University of Portland campus from North Willamette Boulevard. If you're coming from downtown Portland, take Interstate 5 north to North Lombard Street (take the "Lombard West" exit). Drive west on Lombard to North Portsmouth Avenue. Go left on Portsmouth, then turn left again onto Willamette Boulevard. There's a university parking lot on the west side of Willamette. It's accessible from the main entrance road into the campus, near the intersection of North Haven Avenue and Willamette Boulevard.

If you're coming by bus, Tri-Met Bus 40 runs along the edge of the campus on Willamette Boulevard.

Getting Around From the university parking lot beside Pilot House, return to the entrance road, walking past a row of beautifully shaped giant sequoias along the way. Veer left on the entrance road and proceed toward Willamette Boulevard, passing a colorful display of azaleas in the median. Turn right to pace the sidewalk along Willamette Boulevard. You'll be shaded by bigleaf maples as you stroll.

The maples on Willamette Boulevard are the university's oldest planted natives. They were pressed into the soil in 1911. Gaze up at their broad trunks and sturdy branches; you'll realize that these massive trees have done a lot of growing in less than a century. The bigleaf maple is the largest known native maple in the Western United States. It's one of only three of North America's 115 species of maple that grow naturally in Oregon.

Turn right onto a concrete pathway at the intersection of North Fiske Avenue and Willamette. Walk onto the campus, passing a bank of bright azaleas on the right. To the left, a Port Orford cedar stands beside one of Brother Moser's prized camellia bushes. Port Orford cedars are natives of southern Oregon. They're prized as sources of commercial timber. (But don't tell Brother Moser that—he surely planted this one for its beauty!)

Just past the camellia, angle left on the sidewalk and continue toward the south end of the campus. Turn right when the sidewalk dumps you on an asphalt road. You'll have a fine view to the south, with Swan Island in the foreground and the high-rise buildings of downtown Portland in the distance. Skirt the edge of the bluff, with the campus buildings on your right.

Oregon white oaks will offer you their shade as you continue. White oaks are the most common native tree on the University of Portland campus. The most common "weeds" may be the Himalayan blackberries that cover the edges of the bluff. Keep an eye out for the sweet but seedy fruit that helps them earn their keep in the final weeks of August.

Walk beneath the spreading branches of another bigleaf maple as you pass West Hall, and continue toward the river. Pace along the edge of a faculty/staff parking lot, and enter the grass on the outer perimeter of the bluff. Pause to read the bronze plaque on the boulder to the right. It honors the early nineteenth-century exploring duo of Lewis and Clark. Captain Clark ventured as far south as Waud's Bluff during his brief sortie up the Willamette River in 1806.

Plantings near the boulder include camellia bushes, Pacific dogwoods, and giant sequoias. A more recent monument commemorates the Lewis and Clark expedition with an attractive sculpture and another plaque. Pause to study these as you veer left toward the bluff. You might want to sample a juicy salal berry from the bushes nearby if you're visiting in August.

Continue across the grass and walk along the edge of the bluff. There's a small observation point with benches on the left. You'll see the port of Portland shipyards down below, with the broad span of the Fremont Bridge across

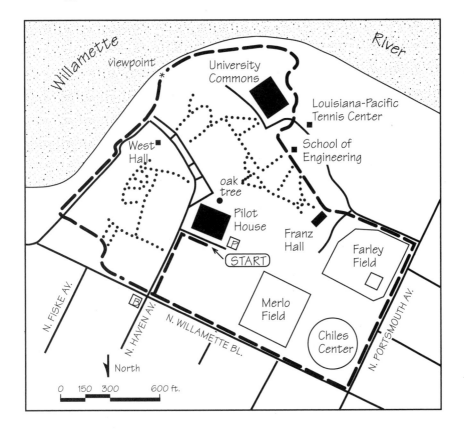

A London planetree catches the morning sun on the University of Portland campus.

the Willamette to the south. There's a nice view of Portland's west hills from here as well.

Leave the observation point, and continue to the west. Watch for several Pacific madrones opposite the chapel. Pacific madrones are evergreens with reddish, peeling bark. They boast small red berries in the fall, and their branches are decorated with white blossoms in the spring.

Pass on the left side of the chapel, and descend gradually through a mixed grove of madrone and oak. Walk to the far western corner of the grass. You'll find a small asphalt path veering to the right. (It's hidden behind a sprinkling of picnic tables.) Turn onto the pathway, then descend a set of stairs beside the university commons. Climb another set of stairs a little farther on, and work your way across the parking lot.

If you're interested in camellias, make a detour to the left to visit the university's Ingram Collection. It contains approximately 200 camellia plants, with more than 50 named varieties. The Louisiana-Pacific Tennis Center will be on your left as you walk across the parking lot.

Veer right to gain a small walkway between the university commons and the School of Engineering. The path is lined with more of Brother Moser's handiwork. Be sure to note the ginkgo tree planted beside the doorway. It's a native of China, often found thriving on the Pacific Coast.

Turn left at the corner of the engineering building, and walk along the building's flower-bedecked front. Admire carefully tended campus lawns on your right and blossoming hydrangeas and azaleas on your left. Continue straight along the sidewalk past the dazzlingly new Franz Hall, then join an intersecting path as you veer toward the left.

Walk along a row of Port Orford cedars and descend a set of stairs. Join the road along the outfield side of the campus baseball field, and walk toward Portsmouth Avenue. At the request of the University of Portland's baseball coach, this outfield fenceline was planted with a variety of conifers in 1982. Twenty years from now, Colorado blue spruce, elkhorn cypress, grand firs, Canadian hemlocks, and a variety of pines will provide a soothing backdrop for the batters' eyes.

Go right on Portsmouth Avenue, and hike past Farley Field to reach the campus sports pavillion, the Chiles Center. You'll pass a lovely Pacific madrone along the way. The university's prized rhododendron species garden rules the rounded perimeter of the Chiles Center. Arrive at Willamette Boulevard, and turn right to walk beneath more bigleaf maples on your way back to your starting point. You can admire the latest addition to the university's sports lineup as you pass Merlo Field (the new soccer stadium) and press on to the campus entry road.

Retrace your steps toward your starting point, but be sure to take the time to swing around the south side of Pilot House. Here, you can pay your respects to the campus's 300-year-old Oregon white oak. It's on the opposite side of the building from Willamette Boulevard, surrounded by an outdoor dining area. Alongside the worthy efforts of the university's many dedicated gardeners, some parts of the campus still remain unchanged. This beautiful tree is testimony to the unequaled gardening prowess of Mother Nature!

♦ 8 ♦
Smith and Bybee Lakes Natural Area

Distance: 1½ miles (round trip)
Estimated time required: 45 minutes
Highlights: Abundant bird life and wetlands wonders
Terrain: Level walking on paved paths; perfect for wheelchairs and strollers
Best time to go: A quiet early morning when the birds are at their best; water
    levels do fluctuate here, so you may want to plan your visit accordingly

Background Driving through the industrial blight along North Marine Drive, you might expect to find factories, truck exhaust, and filling stations. But if you want to find the unexpected here, shun the traffic and the roadside businesses of this busy thoroughfare and explore Smith and Bybee Lakes Natural Area instead.

The 2,000-acre Smith and Bybee Lakes Natural Area is billed by Metro, the regional planning agency that administers and maintains it, as the largest freshwater urban wetlands in the United States. The wetlands area is a part of the Columbia Slough watershed, an 18-mile waterway that flows from Gresham to Kelley Point (Walk 9).

Despite its uniqueness, this natural area is still wonderfully undiscovered and largely undeveloped. It won't stay that way for long. (There are plans afoot to connect Smith and Bybee Lakes to Portland's 40-Mile Loop via a new Peninsula Crossing Trail.) So hurry—come and visit!

The short paved trail from the parking lot will introduce you to Smith and Bybee Lakes. Unpaved trails lead deeper into the wetlands for those who don't mind getting damp and muddy. Bring binoculars for bird watching, and take along a friend or two to keep you company. Children love this trail—it's easy, shaded hiking, with the added bonus of lots and lots of critters to discover.

Getting There To reach the trailhead, take the Marine Drive West exit from Interstate 5. Drive west on North Marine Drive, paralleling Hayden Island and North Portland Harbor. Look for the signed parking area for Smith and Bybee Lakes Natural Area on the south side of the street, just after the road swings left and you cross the railroad tracks on an overpass. The unpaved lot offers portable toilets and an information board.

Tri-Met Bus 6 runs along Marine Drive. Ask for the stop nearest the Smith and Bybee Lakes trailhead.

Getting Around From the southeast end of the parking lot, follow the asphalt trail past tangles of Himalayan blackberries and the pale blue blossoms of chicory. Keep to the right when the trail branches, and arrive at a map of the natural area. Pause to get your bearings, and study the information about resident plants and animals. Be sure to note the 1996 flood-level marker on the signboard's left edge. (Maybe you don't want to visit here after a week or two of rainy days!)

Continue on the wide Interlakes Trail, drinking in the sweet scent of the tall black cottonwoods that rustle overhead. Oregon ash trees toss their shadows on the ground. Beside the path, snowberry bushes and touch-me-nots thrive in late summer. Wildflowers decorate the forest floor in spring, and stinging nettles discourage off-road wandering throughout the year.

Cruise on to a four-way junction, and explore the right branch first. The short detour leads to the shore of an inviting pond. Watch the water for turtles and scan the skies for birds. Return to the junction, and take the path leading left to trace the Observation Loop toward Smith Lake's shore.

Wind through the cottonwoods, and be sure to whisper as you near the

The wonders of nature are right underfoot at Smith and Bybee Lakes Natural Area.

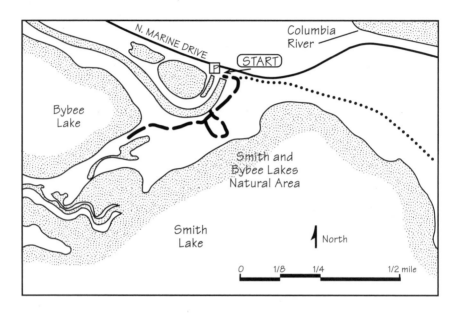

water. As we stood on the metal observation platform one late-summer morning, a great blue heron landed in the lake right in front of us—this despite the presence of a rather boisterous five year old. We saw turtles, too, and a beaver-gnawed log that made us eagerly scan the lake for a glimpse of a furry brown head.

When you're finished watching here, stroll onward with the Observation Loop, pacing an often damp and shady path. If you're walking in autumn, the fallen leaves create vivid compositions as they lie against the dark, wet asphalt. Be sure to listen as you walk. You'll hear the "squeak-plop, squeak-plop" of a host of frogs, fleeing the thunder of your footsteps.

Rejoin the main trail, keeping to the left to continue toward Bybee Lake. Enter more open ground as you approach the sprawling waterway. Dragonflies dance above the flowers in the grassy fields, and the intense symphony of bird songs competes with the sporadic roar of jet engines to fill the air with sound. Reach another observation platform/shelter beside the lake. This marks the end of the natural area's paved trail network—at least for now.

You can wander on into the meadow, tracing unpaved paths along the shore. Watch for great blue herons, red-tailed hawks, belted kingfishers, and coots. Canada geese and bald eagles come in winter, and tree swallows sublet the birdhouse apartments in the trees all year.

If more walking doesn't appeal, you can simply sit in a patch of sunshine and feast your eyes. Contemplate the mist rising off the lake. Watch a bass rise to the surface. Admire the pink blossoms of the water smartweed, cavorting at the water's edge. Smile at the yellow faces of the beggarticks that leap above the grass. Run your fingers over the beaver toothmarks in a discarded log. Or listen to the trucks rumbling past on Marine Drive and hope and pray they'll never build a road or factory in this lovely wild place again.

And when you're finished watching and listening here, retrace your steps back toward the city, following the asphalt ribbon through the trees.

♦ **9** ♦
Kelley Point Park

Distance: 1½ miles (round trip)
Estimated time required: 45 minutes
Highlights: Walk the banks of two great rivers, and watch as they come together
Terrain: A level mix of asphalt and dirt; okay for strollers, limited access for wheelchairs
Best time to go: Try a weekday in the summer; anytime in fall or spring

Background Kelley Point Park is a geographical gem at the northern corner of the city. At Kelley Point, the Willamette River flows into the broad Columbia, losing itself in the larger river's rush toward the Pacific Ocean. If you've ever wondered what becomes of the Willamette after its sedate passage through downtown Portland, come to Kelley Point Park. It offers a wealth of riverside vegetation, fine views of river traffic, and many spots for picnicking and sunbathing.

Kelley Point Park is named for Hall J. Kelley, a New England native who became one of Oregon's most vocal cheerleaders in the first half of the nineteenth century. Kelley launched an unsuccessful drive to establish a city at the confluence of the Willamette and Columbia Rivers. But future Portlanders settled farther south, planting their city on the banks of the Willamette at the site of present-day Tom McCall Waterfront Park.

Kelley Point Park was created by the port of Portland. The once floodprone peninsula was wrested from the river when it was covered with tons of river dredgings. The park that one man envisioned as a city occupies an isolated tip of land today, surrounded by undeveloped flatlands and the slowly spreading industry of the Rivergate Industrial District.

As a result of its location, Kelley Point is often forgotten. In fact, the only time the park is crowded is when the summer sun sends Portlanders scampering for the beaches. In June, July, and August, sunbathers in skimpy suits, teen-agers tuning radios, and picnickers packing in potato salad make Kelley Point a beehive of activity. For much of the rest of the year, the park is quiet.

Choose the side of the park's personality that you'd like to see, and choose the time of year to visit accordingly. Restrooms and picnic facilities are available. Unescorted women shouldn't take this hike in the off-season, since supervision of the grounds is limited or nil.

Getting There To reach Kelley Point Park, take Interstate 5 north to North Marine Drive. Go west on Marine Drive to North Suttle Road (and a sign for Kelley Point), and then drive west on Suttle Road until you reach the turnoff for the park. Keep a sharp eye out for the park sign; the entrance is not well marked. (If you cross the Columbia Slough, you've gone too far.)

Follow a paved road into the park and gain the start of the walk at the second (and final) parking area. There is no public bus service to Kelley Point Park.

Getting Around From the main parking lot, enter the park proper on an asphalt path (behind a yellow metal gate). Walk beneath rustling black cottonwoods as you head toward the Columbia River. Note the park regulations posted on a board beside the trail, then continue straight on the main pathway toward the river.

Ocean-going ships and pleasure boats pass the beaches of Kelley Point Park.

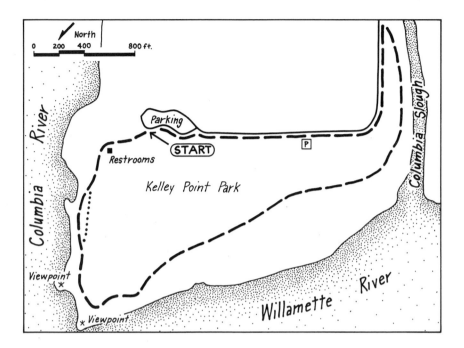

The tiny white blossoms of miner's lettuce light up the trail in May, staking their claim to every bit of open ground available. Pass a restroom building on the left, and angle to the left as you follow the asphalt path around it. You'll get your first glimpse of the Columbia between the cottonwoods as you continue. Take the footpath down to the beach if you can't wait to get a closer look. Otherwise, continue on the paved pathway as you parallel the shoreline. If you're walking in the summer months, you'll share your way with sunbathers and families. The aroma of fried chicken and smoking barbecues radiates from the riverside picnic areas, blotting out the fragrance of the cottonwoods.

Red huckleberry bushes line the path, but clumps of stinging nettles discourage cross-country romps. Continue on beneath tall cottonwoods, and keep to the right as the trail branches. Walk toward the river on the path. Across the Columbia's wide surface, the Washington shoreline peeks above the gray-blue water. If the day is clear, look for flat-topped Mount St. Helens in the distance.

Head for the rusty metal anchor stranded on the shoreline. Although the official confluence of the Willamette and Columbia is not posted at Kelley Point Park, the little sandy bulge ruled by the anchor is the approximate point where the Willamette River joins the Columbia on its journey toward the Pacific Ocean.

You'll see large ocean-going vessels churning up and down the river as you gaze northwest along the broad channel. The Columbia curves northward here, abandoning its westward wandering for a final push toward the Pacific at Astoria. Sailboats, tugs, and barges add their bustle to the river. Pause to watch the traffic for awhile, and perhaps you'll see why Hall J. Kelley thought a commercial city would prosper at this crossroads.

To the west, the shore of Sauvie Island lies just across the water. This section of the park is popular with fishermen, especially when the salmon are running in the spring. Return to the asphalt path, and begin your walk beside the Willamette River. Pass a turnoff for a second viewing area, then pause a little farther on to read a large historical marker.

You'll shake your head in amazement as you read the story of Lewis and Clark's famous journey down the Columbia on their way toward the Pacific Ocean. They sailed past Kelley Point not once but twice, and they never even noticed the Willamette when it joined them! It wasn't until the adventuresome duo talked to some Northwest Indians along the Sandy River that they learned of the Willamette's blending with the Columbia at this spot.

Continue on a gravel roadway past the historical marker. To the left, broad grassy areas attract sunbathers and Frisbee tossers when the weather's hot. Pass a wooden restroom building, and continue beside the river as you walk across the grass. If you'd like to pace the shoreline for awhile, veer right toward the water. For easier hiking, gain another small road at the far end of the grass, and pass beneath more cottonwoods as you parallel the river and walk toward the Columbia Slough.

Watch for wild rabbits in the underbrush on both sides of the road. Great blue herons visit Kelley Point on occasion, and deer and coyotes sometimes wander through. The road follows the line of an old dike. And the beachfront route joins in from the right.

Descend gently to pass an intersecting road, then several side trails, as you continue straight on the sandy road beside the river. Himalayan blackberries lie in tangles everywhere, and a forest of stinging nettles awaits would-be trailblazers. Watch for crimson berries decorating the red elderberry bushes in late spring and summer. These boldly colored berries tempt passing robins. When raw, the red elderberry's fruit is strictly "for the birds," however. The seeds cause diarrhea and vomiting.

When the road angles sharply to the left, turn right to enter a grassy area shaded by the gnarled old trees of an abandoned orchard. (Stay on the road if you're pushing a stroller.) Just across the grass, you can peek over the riverbank for a bird's-eye view of the murky Columbia Slough. If you're tempted to go for a swim—don't—the slough is dangerously polluted.

Continue walking to the far end of the orchard, and regain the paved park entrance road. Go left beside a tangle of Himalayan blackberries to follow the asphalt back toward your car. Or retrace your steps back along the riverfront if you'd like a longer, and more scenic, walk.

◆ 10 ◆
Burntbridge Creek Greenway

Distance: 3 miles (round trip)
Estimated time required: 1 hour and 15 minutes
Highlights: Paved pathways, tall trees, and "hellos" from other hikers make
    this walk a treat
Terrain: Level route on asphalt path; ideal for strollers and wheelchairs
Best time to go: Anytime you're in the neighborhood

Background The walk along Vancouver's Burntbridge Creek Greenway is
as popular with Vancouver residents as Portland's Terwilliger walkway is with
Portlanders. If you live in Vancouver and you haven't explored the Burntbridge
Creek Greenway yet, you're missing out on one of your city's finest walks.
And if you live in Portland and you yearn for a trek that's slightly off the beaten
track, head north soon to explore Burntbridge Creek Greenway.

    This level stroll beside winding little Burntbridge Creek is an ideal out-
ing for families with young children. The paved path beckons strollers, bicycle tires, and training wheels, and the dirt side trails and wild rabbits in the
fields will keep older children occupied for miles. If you visit on a weekend
day, you'll have a lot of company on the greenway.

    Open meadows along the path offer many opportunities for picnicking.

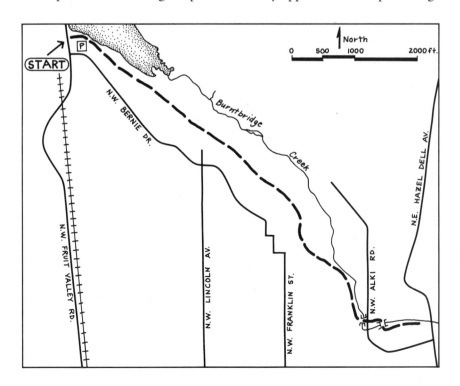

And if you visit Burntbridge Creek Greenway in spring or summer, you'll have wildflowers and butterflies to provide your after-picnic entertainment. Carry water if you plan to linger long. At present, there are no drinking fountains or restrooms on the greenway route.

One note of caution for your walk—Burntbridge Creek Greenway is a bikeway, too. Be prepared to scramble for the side if you hear the whirr of fast-approaching tires. And keep a close eye on your children when the visibility is limited.

Getting There From Portland, drive north on Interstate 5, and take the 39th Street exit past downtown Vancouver. Go west on East 39th Street to its intersection with Northwest Fruit Valley Road. Turn right here, and follow Fruit Valley Road to Northwest Bernie Drive. Go right on Bernie Drive, and then veer left just afterward into the small parking area beside the trailhead. There are slots for 12 to 15 cars here, and there are picnic tables and garbage cans, as well.

Vancouver's public transit system serves Burntbridge Creek Greenway with C-Tran Bus 2.

Getting Around Leave the parking area via the path on the northeast corner (wheelchair and stroller access is from the corner of Bernie Drive and Fruit Valley Road), and walk down a steep stair-stepped incline to gain the paved Discovery Trail. Go right on the trail, with the backed-up waters of Burntbridge Creek shimmering on your left. This placid pond area is popular with fishermen of all ages.

You'll pass a handsome walnut tree after about 100 yards. The path is lined with Himalayan blackberry bushes, and the fruit is ripe and ready for sampling in late summer. Vine maples crowd along the sides, competing with thimbleberry bushes for surplus sun. You'll see a vast variety of deciduous trees as you walk, and Douglas firs and western hemlocks add their contributions to the many shades of green.

Continue east along the level pathway. The abundant trees keep the pavement blanketed with shade. If you're walking on a weekend day, you'll have a lot of company to keep you entertained. Weekdays are a little quieter on Burntbridge Creek Greenway, but dedicated walkers will be pacing out their miles, rain or shine.

Watch for several red elderberry bushes as you walk. In the spring, fringe cups are abundant on the trailsides. You'll know them by their small, cup-shaped blossoms growing on tall green stems. Sword and bracken ferns add to the forest ground cover, greedily absorbing the drops of sunlight spilled by tall red alders.

You'll notice many unpaved pathways tempting hikers off toward the

Vancouver's Burntbridge Creek Greenway attracts scores of enthusiastic walkers.

creek. Tiptoe, if you go. You might get lucky and surprise a great blue heron. There's nothing quite like the thrill of watching one of these gangly creatures struggle into flight.

After about ⅓ mile, watch for a lightning-scarred Douglas fir trunk on the right side of the trail. It's interesting to see how the interior of the trunk was blackened by the searing bolt. Red huckleberry bushes are woven through the forest just beyond. If you decide to do a little berry picking on your walk, be forewarned—there are lots of stinging nettles in the underbrush.

Watch for a beautiful old Oregon white oak tree on the left side of the trail, about 200 yards beyond the Douglas fir stump. The spreading branches of the oak reach out to shade the trail, and the flat space within the leafy hub of limbs looks absolutely perfect for a child's treehouse. This old oak is a composition that deserves long study. It's one of nature's masterpieces, growing in a vast outdoor museum.

Continue on the paved pathway, and watch for wild strawberries in early summer. In June, crimson columbine hangs beside the trail, its bright blossoms looking like blazing red and yellow lanterns. You'll come in beside a grassy meadow as you follow the course of Burntbridge Creek east. Several overgrown pathways lead out into the grass. If you're a wildflower lover, wander out into the meadow in the springtime. Blue-pod lupine is abundant here, and you'll spot the low-lying purple blossoms of tough-leaved irises.

Return to the paved pathway, and continue. You'll pass a fragrant bank of wild roses on the left, and you'll see trailing blackberries that sprinkle the ground with small white blossoms in late May. On the right, a deep forest of Douglas firs and western red cedars throws its shade across the trail. The tiny white flowers of miner's lettuce dot the ground in April. And northern inside-out flowers add their delicate white blossoms to the forest show in May.

Things open up again as you walk beside a grassy field inhabited by battalions of bouncing wild rabbits. Then more Douglas firs take over, shading a cool glen where vanilla leaf and northern inside-out flowers turn their faces toward the sun. If you visit in March or early April, you'll see trilliums among the ferns.

Descend gently from the forested glen and pass beneath a low set of powerlines. Skirt along a sunny meadow where yellow buttercups set the grass ablaze with color on April afternoons. You'll pass several gnarled old pear trees as you wind across the field. And the murmur of Interstate 5 will begin to whisper in your ears as you continue.

Wander beside the chortling waters of Burntbridge Creek, and cross the little waterway on a wooden bridge. Cross a small asphalt road (Alki Road), and continue on the bikeway.

Watch for an English holly bush on the right side of the trail as you re-cross Burntbridge Creek on a second wooden bridge. You'll come to another road; continue to the end of the greenway at Northeast Hazel Dell Avenue. Retrace your steps along the creek to regain your starting point.

◆ 11 ◆
Salmon Creek Greenway

Distance: 6 miles (round trip)
Estimated time required: 2½ hours
Highlights: A wonderful creekside walk that's perfect for families; don't miss the blackberries!
Terrain: Paved, level trail; great for strollers, wheelchairs, rollerblades, bikes . . .
Best time to go: Anytime you want some exercise

Background Salmon Creek Greenway is a narrow strip of unpaved earth, set beside a meandering waterway, and hemmed in by ridgetop housing developments and sprawling neighborhoods. It's home to fish and frogs, birds and reptiles, rabbits and butterflies. Wildflowers blossom here. Black cottonwoods stand tall beside the water. And the breeze in this green valley is sweet, unspoiled by the city that surrounds it.

A grandfather and grandson sample sweet blackberries beside Salmon Creek.

Salmon Creek County Park consists of 403 acres along the Salmon Creek watershed. The park area was obtained in 1975 through a generous land donation, but it's only recently that the 3-mile-long streamside path was completed. That path is a testimony to Clark County's ongoing commitment to establishing parks and trails that preserve and access nature.

The creek that lends the park and greenway its name flows 33 miles from its origin on the slopes of Spotted Deer and Little Elkhorn Mountains to the Lake River, then empties into Vancouver Lake. Spend an afternoon walking the path beside Salmon Creek. You won't find untamed wilderness on this urban greenway, but you will find a breath of nature, and that breath is sweet and full of life.

Getting There From downtown Portland, head north on Interstate 5, and take the 99th Street Exit (Exit 5) in Vancouver. Keep to the right from the exit, then go left at the light to get on Northeast Highway 99. You'll go left again on 117th. (Note the sign for Salmon Creek County Park.) Go right soon afterward to enter the popular park set beside Klineline Pond. A slight fee is charged for park users.

If you want to hike for free and you don't require the restrooms, swimming area, and picnic tables at this tidy county park, drive about ⅓ mile past the park entrance on 117th Street, and turn right into the Salmon Creek Sports Complex. You can begin hiking from here.

The Salmon Creek Greenway Trail can be accessed from C-Tran Bus 6 (on 117th) and C-Tran Bus 21 (at trail's end on Northwest 36th Avenue).

Getting Around Set out from the far end of the paved parking area on a wide asphalt path. If you're hiking in August, the enormous banks of Himalayan

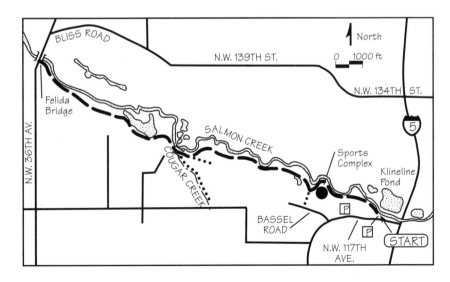

blackberries beside the path may delay your start a bit. Don't worry if you dribble a little—after a day spent exploring this trail in late summer, we came to the conclusion that juice-stained T-shirts are a badge of honor here!

Sweet-smelling black cottonwoods line the way as you draw close to Salmon Creek. You'll hear the chortle of the water mixed with the songs of birds as you stroll onward. Pass the alternate trailhead parking area after ¼ mile, and wind past a Little League complex before continuing beside the creek. A host of use trails lead toward the water. Look for the orange blossoms of touch-me-not in late summer.

You'll appreciate the level walking if the day is hot, as there's not much shade along this route. Of course, you can always stop for breathers among the blackberry bushes. If you're walking with children, do take care. There's quite a bit of European bittersweet (also known as "nightshade") scattered in with the blackberry bushes. This plant's fat red berries are poisonous to humans, so be sure to supervise the picking.

Tall wild carrot blossoms bob beside the path as you continue, and the leaves of willows and cottonwoods whisper above the water. Tiny frogs scramble to escape passing hikers, diving for the water in a symphony of plops.

After about 1 mile, the trail cuts through a vast, grassy meadow. Wildflowers are abundant here in spring. Bring along a flower identification book or a loaded camera, and have at it! We spotted the yellow faces of beggarticks and the white blossoms of wappato when we visited in late summer.

Pass the 1½-mile point in the middle of flat and open hiking. The majestic flyby of a startled heron made things exciting, just when we were getting bored. You'll regain the company of Salmon Creek as you stroll on, its disposition now placid, its route meandering.

Keep to the right as the trail branches, and revel in the shade offered by a maple-covered hillside. The blossoms of false Solomon's seal glow in the darkness, and sword ferns probe the shadows with their sunlight-seeking blades. Later in the year, white snowberries cling to drooping bushes and orange blossoms of touch-me-not hang like tiny lanterns on green stems.

Cross little Cougar Creek on a sturdy bridge, and reenter the open meadow. Grand houses hover on the ridges above the waterway. Tall Douglas firs keep to the high ground, too, as if afraid to get their feet wet. Another patch of shade graces the 2-mile mark, as the trail nestles in beside the hill once more. Watch for wild roses and bracken ferns as you continue. If you're not totally satiated with blackberries by now, there are more.

A bench-equipped viewing area invites you to pause and picnic before trail's end. Or simply sit and do a bit of nature watching from here. Rollerbladers, cyclists, and joggers will flow past as you ponder. Press on toward the end of the greenway trail. Encroaching housing developments attempt to spoil the ambience of the creek during the final ½ mile. Feast your eyes on nature instead of backyard furniture, and wander on.

Reach the end of the greenway trail at Northwest 36th Avenue. There's shoulder parking here, if you want to establish a car shuttle. Don't miss the great view of Mount Hood above the winding creek as you turn back to hike toward your starting point.

◆ **12** ◆
Lacamas Park

Distance: 3 miles (round trip)
Estimated time required: 1½ hours
Highlights: An invigorating tromp through a lovely, varied forest; glimpses of two tantalizing creeks
Terrain: Unpaved trails lead through roller-coaster forestland; no wheelchairs or strollers
Best time to go: Weekdays in spring or summer for wildflowers, wading, and solitude; anytime in fall for fabulous maple leaves

Background Lacamas Park is a large recreational forestland administered by a loose conglomeration of public organizations, including Clark County, Washington. Located in the fast-growing city of Camas, it's a bit of a drive from the urban centers of Portland and Vancouver. But Lacamas Park is certainly worth the trip.

The park offers an extensive (if somewhat confusing) trail network, with opportunities to view a variety of trees, wildflowers, and bird and animal life. The two creeks that trickle through the forest, Lacamas Creek and Woodburn Creek, form lovely pools and waterfalls that invite an entire day of exploration. Add in opportunities for "plunk-it-in" fishing from the banks of Round Lake and for play and picnicking in the developed part of the park, and you'll have the makings of plenty of family fun.

One word of warning for hikers who come here—currently, there is virtually no signage on the trails. Especially on the trails close to Round Lake, heavy mountain-bike traffic has created a tangled mess of junctions. Come prepared to dodge irresponsible cyclists. Come resigned to a bit of routefinding confusion. But do come. You'll be glad you visited this gem of a forest.

Getting There To find Lacamas Park, take Highway 14 east from Vancouver and the Sam Jackson (Interstate 205) Bridge. Follow signs for Camas, then take Exit 12 for the Camas Business Loop. Wind through the city's downtown hub, and turn left on Northeast Garfield Street. This becomes Road 500 (Northeast Everett Street).

Stay with Everett Street up the hill away from town, then watch for a

Mushrooms thrive in the forested recesses of Lacamas Park.

paved parking area on the right side of the road. It's marked by a sign for Lacamas Park. If this surprisingly small parking lot is full, there's an overflow area a little farther on (turn right on Leonard Road).

Lacamas Park is served by C-Tran Bus 33.

Getting Around Swing to the right from the small parking area to begin a counterclockwise walk along the shore of Round Lake. You'll see a play structure, picnic tables, and restrooms as you enter the shaded park proper. Perhaps you'll wonder, as we did, why this is called Lacamas Park when it's on Round Lake. (Lacamas Lake is across the road.) Best guess—the two lakes are connected, and Lacamas Lake is a whole lot bigger than Round Lake. Besides, the name is a lot more interesting.

Pace a lakeside path beneath tall Douglas firs, enjoying views out across the water. Vine maples write poetry with leaves and sunlight overhead. You'll see bracken ferns, salal, and Oregon grape bushes before you're out of the "civilized" park. There's so much more ahead.

Cross a wood-plank walkway that's often lined with fishermen, and glance to the right onto tiny Mill Pond. Angle left to pace another walkway across Round Lake's outlet. Here, water goes over a spillway and splashes down through a rocky ravine, rescuing Lacamas Creek from its brief life as a lake. (If you're hiking when the lake level is high, you may have difficulty crossing here. Please refer to the map for alternate access to the forest trails.)

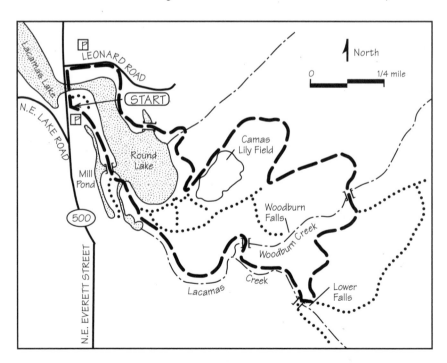

Gaze down on the dark pools and smooth rocks formed by Lacamas Creek's passage, then walk onward. Shun the first trail to the right (it's for those unable to resist the water's charms), and take the second path. You'll pace a wide trail through thick trees. Thimbleberries, trailing blackberries, and red huckleberries offer new opportunities to stray from your commitment to hiking. Nibble a bit, then press on.

Walk in the shade of red alders and Douglas firs, then dive right off the wide path to follow a smaller trail above Lacamas Creek's lovely chasm. Hike in the company of the creek's subdued symphony, letting your eyes soak in the beauty of tiny falls and rounded rocks. If your toes urge you to do another type of soaking, please be cautious. The water-smoothed stones are very slippery.

Pause at an overlook to gaze at another of Lacamas Creek's water-colored canvases, then continue across an open, rocky knob sprinkled with Oregon white oaks. Descend gently for a time, then dive downhill steeply to cross tiny Woodburn Creek on a wooden footbridge. Wonderful western red cedars inhabit the valley floor, their shaggy-barked trunks soaring gracefully toward lofty branches.

Rejoin Lacamas Creek here as you follow the trail gently downhill. The air is cool and sweet in the gully bottom, and ferns and wildflowers are abundant in the shade of regal cedars. You'll reach a long bridge spanning the creek at Lower Falls. Walk out on the span for a view of rocks and rivulets. (An alternate access trail joins from outside the park proper here.)

Return to your trail beside the water, staying with the upper route along the hillside. It's wide and sprinkled with gravel. Climb briefly, then veer left just before the main trail heads downhill again. Ascend on a narrow footpath through red-alder shade. Note the white patches of lichens on the trunks of the trees.

You'll endure a steady uphill push for awhile, picking up the company of occasional western hemlocks. We spotted some enormous mushrooms here. At last, the trail levels out again. Watch for impressive Douglas fir stumps scattered throughout the secondary forest of alder and maple. When this forest was logged many years ago, the demise of the Douglas firs allowed the fast-growing deciduous trees to move in.

Your small trail will lead you to a much wider service road (probably one of the old logging routes). Go left along the old roadway, and watch for a toppled Douglas fir, overcome by blackberries. Cross Woodburn Creek on a wooden bridge, then look for another Douglas fir—this giant is still standing—and climb again.

The terrain levels shortly afterward, as you continue to hike the old roadbed. Look for a trail to the right, marked by a "no bikes" logo and a "Natural Area" designation. Follow the trail through a red alder thicket, where an understory of Oregon grape offers enough tart berries to pucker up anyone. Cheer up the "sourpusses" in your group with a sample of the ripe salal berries

decorating the trail in August and September. They are much sweeter than the Oregon grape.

A gentle uphill climb leads to a hilltop meadow. This protected corner of the forest is the home of great numbers of lovely deep-blue camas flowers, blooming in the spring. A perennial bulb, camas was an important food source for Pacific Northwest tribes. The bulbs were dug with sticks and steamed in pits. Though camas was a primary source of nourishment for Native Americans, you'll undoubtedly appreciate it more for the way its beauty nourishes your soul. Even the well-traveled explorer Merriwether Lewis took note of the striking camas blossoms, writing in his journal of the vast fields of flowers he saw while on his trip through the Pacific Northwest.

Hike across the oak-dotted hilltop, pausing often to admire an array of wildflowers, then watch for a small trail diving downhill to the right. Endure a steep descent, led onward by the shimmer of the lake between the trees. Regain the service road and swing right, negotiating a bit of up-and-down hiking, then finish with a gentle descent to the shore of Round Lake.

Continue with your counterclockwise loop, passing a tiny marsh area on your way to the paved Leonard Road. Note Lacamas Park's overflow parking lot as you walk on, then turn left along the shoulder of Everett Street. Cross the causeway between Lacamas Lake and Round Lake, and arrive at the parking lot and your start.

Ferns are abundant beneath the tall trees in Lacamas Park.

Northeast Portland

The Grotto

Distance: 1 mile (round trip)
Estimated time required: 40 minutes
Highlights: Beautiful forest setting and a network of flower-lined paths
Terrain: Paved, level pathways, great for strollers and wheelchairs
Best time to go: Choose a spring or summer weekday to avoid the crowds

Background The Grotto (otherwise known as The Sanctuary of Our Sorrowful Mother) is a wonderful place to walk when you're yearning for a silent stroll. You won't have to contend with cars or bicycles in this tree-shaded retreat. No dogs are allowed. And even the joggers leave The Grotto's paths to those with a slower pace. Somehow, speed just doesn't seem appropriate here. And radios and loud conversations are definitely out of place. At The Grotto, silence is the rule rather than the exception.

The Grotto is a 64-acre outdoor sanctuary staffed by the Order of the Servants of Mary. The land was obtained from Burlington Northern Railroad in 1923, and about a dozen brothers, priests, and nuns reside in the small monastery on the upper level of the parklike enclave. A full-time staff of more than 20 individuals runs the gift shop and keeps the gardens tended. The Grotto's costs are met through donations, gift shop profits, and revenue from the elevator to the upper level.

The Grotto attracts more than 100,000 visitors each year. You'll probably hear several foreign languages spoken there on a summer afternoon. There is no admission charge to the grounds, but there is a fee for the roundtrip elevator ride to the upper level. (Children under six are free.) The elevator runs daily from 9 A.M. to 4:30 or 5:30 P.M., depending on the season.

Tucked into the base of east Portland's Rocky Butte, The Grotto boasts a lovely mix of wild forest and well-tended flower beds. Sword ferns and trilliums duel beneath tall Douglas firs and droopy-headed western hemlocks. Roses and rhododendrons add splashes of crimson and purple and orange to the emerald lawns. The scent of damp earth and fallen needles permeates the air. The songs of birds trickle down the pathways. And patches of sunlight filter through the trees, making winter-weary hearts rejoice.

Although the pathways through The Grotto are sprinkled with religious statuary and the center of attention is a cliff-walled outdoor sanctuary, one

Vanilla leaf flourishes beside the shaded pathways of The Grotto.

certainly doesn't have to be Catholic to enjoy this place. The Grotto's natural beauty is something any walker will appreciate. Simply put, The Grotto is a heavenly place to stroll.

Getting There The Grotto lies just to the northeast of the intersection of Northeast 82nd Avenue and Northeast Sandy Boulevard. Drive northeast on Sandy from 82nd Avenue, and look for The Grotto's large entrance sign on the right side of the road. Turn right onto a paved entrance road bordered by a pair of giant sequoias. There's a large parking lot just inside the grounds.

If you're arriving by bus, Tri-Met Bus 12 runs past The Grotto on Northeast Sandy Boulevard. There's a stop right beside the entrance.

Getting Around Begin your visit to The Grotto with a look inside the glass-enclosed Welcome Center. You can pick up a brochure and map here, and you may want to return at hike's end to browse for books, cards, brownies, or espresso. If you plan to visit The Grotto's upper level on this trip, you can purchase elevator tokens at the desk before you start your walk. (Currently, tokens are also available at the old information center building at the rear of the outdoor sanctuary.)

Leave the Welcome Center, and go right to climb a set of steps. (Visitors with wheelchairs or strollers can backtrack to the southeast corner of the parking lot and gain the trail toward the right from there.) At the top of the stairs, veer right to follow an asphalt path along The Grotto's Stations of the Cross. Please be courteous toward other visitors, some of whom you'll see in meditation at the shrines.

Heavy-branched Douglas firs shade the way as you begin to walk. Rhododendrons paint the pathways pink and purple in the spring, and sword ferns carpet the forest floor in green. Watch for wildflowers as you continue. Vanilla leaf is plentiful beside the path in spring. The plant's white blossoms stand erect above low leaves, looking much like a chubby pipecleaner. Vanilla leaf was popular with pioneer women in the past. They used the fragrant greenery as a potpourri.

If you're walking in April or May, you'll have scores of early wildflowers to keep you company. Look for fringe cups sprinkled among the ferns. Trilliums are here, as well. And northern inside-out flowers dangle from thin, green stems.

Western hemlocks compete with Douglas firs as The Grotto's predominant tree. Both species are dressed in lovely frocks of lime-green needles in the spring. New growths decorate the borders of their branches, standing out in sharp contrast to the old. Look for shorter needles and a droopy top to differentiate the western hemlock from Oregon's state tree.

More ferns and a lot of Oregon grape line the path as you walk. Snatches

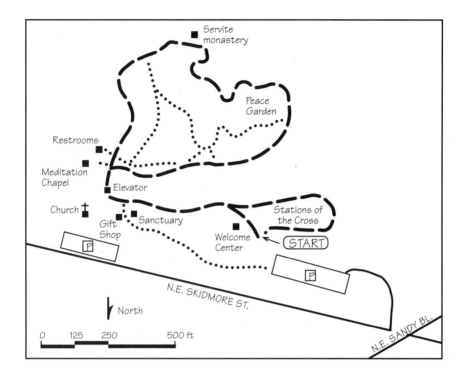

Servite monastery

Peace Garden

Restrooms

Meditation Chapel

Elevator

Church

Gift Shop

Sanctuary

Welcome Center

Stations of the Cross

START

N.E. SKIDMORE ST.

North

0   125   250   500 ft

N.E. SANDY BL.

of traffic noise from Northeast Sandy Boulevard drift south through the trees. And occasionally a low-flying plane bound for Portland International Airport will rumble overhead, shattering the forest's spell. Stay on the winding pathway, angling left to climb gently uphill. Before long, you will have looped back toward the east.

More western hemlocks gather to block out the sun. These trees often grow in dense, dark groves. Their wood is used for pulp and as a source of cellulose. English holly bushes add their prickly leaves to the trailside menagerie of plants. Continue on the asphalt path, passing several ivy-covered shrines.

Red elderberry bushes grow beside the trail. In the fall, they add splashes of crimson to the glut of green. Walk gently downhill. You'll pass plenty of false Solomon's seal if you're hiking in the spring. Press your nose against one of the fluffy blossoms. The fragrance is as sweet as any rose's scent. Another spring blossom lining The Grotto's paths is Siberian lettuce.

Descend to a junction where the footpath from the parking lot joins in. The way is lined with rhododendrons as you continue straight ahead. Strains of music from the outdoor sanctuary will tiptoe down to meet you on the trail. Pass a shrine with a hillside waterfall. Look for lovely maidenhair ferns growing around the lower pool.

On the left, a handsome statue of Christ is framed by rhododendrons. Enter the outdoor sanctuary, and make your way across. If there's a service going on, be sure to skirt the rear. The Grotto gets its name from the natural amphitheater of stone that forms the south wall of the outdoor sanctuary. The cliff is 110 feet high, and a replica of Michelangelo's *Pietà* rules the fern-covered rock face. Gaze upward at the summit of the cliff. That's where the ten-story elevator will deposit you, if you decide to make the trip.

If the fee for the journey to the top has you dragging your feet a bit, you can simply wander The Grotto's lower level another time or two. If you'd like to combine this hike with a rougher forest scramble, you can explore the trails along the northeast edge of Rocky Butte (between the steep rock slopes and Interstate 205). You'll find a trail behind The Grotto's church, at the far end of the lower parking area. It's possible to follow this trail about ½ mile around the butte, then up the hill to the Portland Bible College campus.

To continue The Grotto walk, take the elevator to the upper level. Emerge from the elevator, and pause at the flower-filled Grotto Garden Plaza. This plaza and the beautiful Meditation Chapel to the left are part of a recent flurry of construction and renovation here. On a clear day, the view from the Medi-tation Chapel is glorious.

Angle right from the Garden Plaza and stop at a small map of the upper grounds mounted on a board beside the trail. Continue on the path leading to the left, following the white arrows painted on small signboards along the asphalt-covered route.

This part of The Grotto isn't as forested as the lower level. Open grassy areas and overflowing flower beds lie among the trees. It's well worth a visit in the summer, however. The plants are varied and colorful, and the soaring trees are magnificent. You'll be impressed by the size and abundance of Colorado blue spruce trees on this upper tier. Giant sequoias are well repre-sented, too, as are the ever-present western hemlocks, western red cedars, and Douglas firs.

Continue through a grassy grove made colorful with azaleas, camellias, and rhododendrons. Squirrels dash across the lawns, providing welcome dis-tractions for excited children, and bird songs are everywhere, mingled with the chortle of the fountains. Stay with the white-arrow route, and savor the view of maple-shaded wildflowers in fern-lined beds. If you have the time and inclination, The Grotto's quiet grounds would be a wonderful place to wander with your nose inside a plant identification book.

Walk on where wild bleeding hearts hang heavy with their pale pink flowers in the spring, and fringe cups and trilliums compete for the flower lover's gaze. Curve to the right, and follow the white arrows toward The Grotto's small stone monastery. Just before you reach the monastery, watch for a thick-trunked giant sequoia on the left side of the trail. The sequoia's reddish bark is deeply grooved, and it would take two sets of outstretched arms to reach around the tree's massive base. This hefty specimen makes it easy to understand how the giant sequoia got its other common name—bigtree.

Continue on the pathway in front of the monastery, walking beside a vibrant rose garden. The Grotto's Servite monastery was built in 1936. The Servite order itself dates back to 1233. Walk past the front of the building, then loop back around the western edge of the rose garden and take the first footpath to the left. Pass between bushy rhododendrons, and angle left again to enter a relatively recent addition to The Grotto's grounds—the Peace Garden.

Walk beneath scattered bigleaf maples to arrive beside a small artificial pond. The murmur of the water provides a welcome muffler for the traffic noise from 82nd Avenue. Follow a weaving pathway through the landscaped grounds, walking past ferns and rhododendrons, azaleas and ornamental maple trees. Join an older asphalt path as you leave the Peace Garden, and keep left along the bluff to begin your walk back toward the elevator. The sunlight slanting through the trees is lovely in the morning hours.

Take a small detour to the left at the lofty statue of Mary, and stroll to the edge of the cliff to gaze down on the outdoor sanctuary. If heights make your stomach squirm, look out into the distance instead. The view to the north is lovely on a hazeless day. Look for the Washington peaks of Mount St. Helens, Mount Rainier, and Mount Adams. Closer in, you'll see the blue-gray Columbia River, making its journey west.

If you have children along, use caution here. But be sure to linger long enough to let them watch a plane take off from Portland International Airport.

If you brought a sandwich or a book, you might decide to find a spot in the grass and enjoy The Grotto for another quiet hour. Then turn back toward the elevator and your starting point.

◆ 14 ◆
Rose City Golf Course

Distance: 2¼ miles (round trip)
Estimated time required: 45 minutes
Highlights: Pleasant city stroll with views of trees and fairways
Terrain: Unpaved pathway with scattered stairs; okay for strollers, no wheelchairs
Best time to go: Choose a weekday morning when the golf course traffic is
   lightest

Background Looking for a pleasant city walk where you can stretch your legs without fighting cars and bus exhaust? This hike around Rose City Golf Course may be just the stroll you're looking for. Take a trip around the perimeter of this 18-hole public course, and you'll walk beside green fairways and tall trees. You'll chuckle at squirrels as they bounce across the lawns. You'll admire well-kept yards and handsome homes. And you'll share your way with local joggers, hikers, and dog walkers as you explore.

As with most of the golf courses in the Portland area, Rose City Golf Course is heavily posted with signs prohibiting trespassing. Walkers aren't allowed to use the golf course proper, as they are at Glendoveer (see Walk 15). Fortunately, though, there's a smooth footpath worn into the grass just outside the golf course fence, and it's easy to enjoy the course's quiet and beauty from a legal distance.

Although you won't have to worry about cars or deal with many street crossings on this walk, please keep an eye out for errant golf balls. You'll be walking close to fairways almost the entire way. Always watch the strokes of nearby golfers, and always be prepared to duck.

Getting There From downtown Portland, drive east on Interstate 84 (the Banfield Freeway) and take the Northeast 68th Avenue exit; you'll emerge onto Northeast Halsey Street. Continue east to Northeast 74th Avenue. Turn left on 74th, cross over the freeway, and continue to Northeast Tillamook Street, the southern boundary of Rose City Golf Course. There is a lot of on-street parking along the south side of Tillamook. Our loop begins at the intersection of Tillamook and Northeast 72nd Avenue, just opposite the course's clubhouse and parking lot.

If you're coming by bus, Tri-Met Bus 77 runs along Halsey Street. Get off at 74th Avenue, and walk three blocks north on 74th to reach Rose City Golf Course. A second option is to take Tri-Met Bus 72 along Northeast 82nd Avenue. Ask for the stop at Tillamook, and walk west on Tillamook to join the golf course loop at Northeast 78th Avenue.

Getting Around Begin your hike by walking east on Tillamook Street from the intersection with 72nd Avenue. There's a nice footpath paralleling the golf course on the north side of Tillamook. If the weather is very wet, you may want to pace the sidewalks on the south side of the street instead. You'll lose a bit of the golf course view, but your feet will stay dry a little longer.

If you're sticking with the footpath, walk beneath the spreading branches of maple trees as you start out. In the spring, a colorful collection of azaleas brightens the west end of the fairway. Watch for the regal shapes of a handful of giant sequoias out in the grass. It's easy to tell these cone-shaped trees are members of the redwood family; their rough-barked trunks have a notice-able reddish hue.

Leave the shade of the maples for a moment, and exchange their leaf-covered limbs for the drooping branches of a deodar cedar. Note the way the needles sprout from the bark in light green tufts. This native of the Himalayas is highly valued in India for its strong, aromatic wood. Since its introduction

A local walker makes the trek around the Rose City Golf Course.

to North America, the tree's popularity in California has given it a second name—the California Christmas tree.

Continue on beneath more maples. Watch for three Port Orford cedars beside the fence. These trees are named for Port Orford, Oregon. They are abundant in the southwest corner of the state, and their fragrant wood is exported to Japan for use in the construction of religious shrines.

Traffic on Tillamook Street is fairly steady but not unpleasant. You'll probably count more golfers than cars if you're walking on a sunny week-end day. Watch for a group of horsechestnut trees just across the fairway as you continue. Large cream-colored blossoms make them especially beautiful in May. Descend slightly toward 75th Avenue, and enjoy an excellent view of Mount Hood, if the day is clear. Then enjoy level walking once again.

Walk beside Douglas firs as you near the east end of the golf course, and turn left onto 78th Avenue to continue along the edge of the fence. Watch for squirrels bounding through the branches of the trees as you head north on 78th. You'll walk beside a row of European white birches, then veer right onto unpaved Northeast Thompson Street. Rising over the houses to the east, the tree-covered mound of Rocky Butte leaves its imprint on the Portland skyline.

Follow Thompson Street to the east end of the golf course, then veer left through an opening in the chain-link fence. You'll walk north through the athletic fields of Madison High School as you parallel the golf course fence. Stroll beneath the heavy-laden branches of a horsechestnut tree as you continue. The horsechestnut is another one of Portland's "imported" trees. It's actually a native of southeastern Europe. The tree owes its unusual name to the practice of Turkish veterinarians. They ground up the seeds and fed them to horses as a cure for equine coughing spells.

Cross the west end of the high-school track, and climb a set of stairs beside the football grandstand. Veer left to skirt the bottom of the Madison

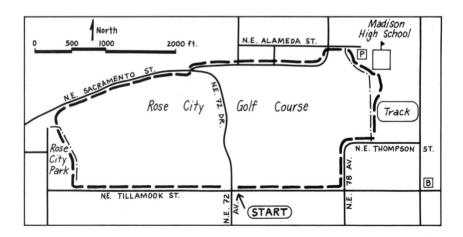

gymnasium, then go right around the corner of the building and climb a second set of stairs. Angle left through a parking area, climbing gently as you continue. You'll have views down onto the golf course as you walk.

Work your way northward through the parking lot, and turn left onto Northeast Alameda Street to leave the high-school grounds. Go left again at the intersection with Northeast 77th Avenue, and curve back toward the upper edge of the golf course on Northeast Sacramento Street. Keep to the sidewalk on the north side of Sacramento until the intersection with 72nd Avenue, then cross carefully to gain the grassy bluff above the golf course and enjoy a bird's-eye view.

The dull roar of the Banfield Freeway will drift up to your ears as you continue. Just before the intersection of Sacramento Street and Northeast 70th Avenue, dive downhill on a wide dirt path to reach Northeast 72nd Drive, the golf course road. Cross carefully, and regain the footpath on the west side of the street. Continue west along the hillside, walking between Sacramento above and the golf course fairways just below.

If you're pushing a stroller or walking in wet weather, you may want to stay on Sacramento Street rather than descend to the hillside path. You'll be a little closer to the traffic as you pace the north side of the golf course, but you'll have fine views and smoother walking for awhile. Descend a set of old stone stairs at the west end of the golf course to rejoin our route.

The hillside path skirts beneath Douglas firs and assorted pines as you leave 72nd Drive. Watch for giant sequoias lining the fairways to the left. In the spring, wildflowers hide in bunches of long grass. The bright white faces of wild carrot blossoms smile in the sunshine all summer long, while ripe Himalayan blackberries make the hillside particularly fragrant in August and September. Of course, golf-ball pickings are excellent in every season.

Gaze out across the golf course to the south. You'll see the bulge of volcanic Mount Tabor in the distance (Walk 17). Be sure to keep an eye on nearby golfers, too. You'll be very close to Rose City's fairways on this section of the route, so be prepared to dodge an errant ball if you hear a shout.

Stay on the lower path as secondary trails trickle down the hillside to the right. Come in beside a chain-link fence as you approach the west end of the golf course, and emerge at a set of stairs. (This is where the Sacramento route joins in.) Descend to a gravel path, and begin your walk along the west edge of the golf course, making your way through the shaded lawns of Rose City Park.

Hug the boundary of the golf course as you continue south. The park offers restrooms, drinking fountains, and swingsets, if you need a break. Watch the antics of the squirrels playing in the grass as you walk past a row of western red cedars and Port Orford cedars planted beside the fence. Douglas firs tower above two almost sunless tennis courts, and softball fields inhabit the open flatlands beyond the trees.

Gain a dirt footpath through the grass, and stay beside the fence as you pass several twisted-trunk Scotch pines. The building to the right is Charles A. Rice Elementary School. Emerge onto Tillamook Street again, and turn left onto the footpath along the shoulder to make your way back toward your starting point.

◆ 15 ◆
Glendoveer Fitness Course

Distance: 2 miles (round trip)
Estimated time required: 40 minutes
Highlights: A 2-mile romp with a wonderful assortment of Portland pedestrians
Terrain: Level hiking on a sawdust-covered path; no wheelchairs, heavy-duty strollers might be okay
Best time to go: Mudless paths are a great option for wet-weather wandering

Background If you haven't walked the 2-mile exercise loop around Glendoveer Golf Course yet, you're really missing something. Oh, it's not that this trail is breathtakingly beautiful or romantically remote. It's not that it's particularly unusual, and it's certainly not that it's unknown. One look at the near-constant flow of people striding around Glendoveer's perimeter, and you'll realize you aren't the first walker to try this route.

So what is it that makes the Glendoveer Fitness Course so special? People—lots of them. Few walks in Portland are so well loved and used (and used and used and used). Gray-haired retirees and baby-toting moms, recuperating heart patients and reducing dieters, fleet-footed runners and slow-stepping stragglers—all types of people find their way there. Glendoveer is Portland pedestrians on parade.

The Multnomah County Parks Services Division maintains this pleasant path around the 36-hole golf course. Somehow, Glendoveer seems more like a circular neighborhood than a 2-mile exercise route. Regular walkers know each other's medical histories, workout schedules, and lap times. People greet each other by name as they pass on the trail. There are no dogs or bicycles allowed, and there's virtually no litter. There's even an official pedestrians' parking lot (with two porta-toilets and a drinking fountain for the crowds).

If you bring children on this walk, they'll think they're hiking at the zoo. The forested fringes of the path are populated by bounding squirrels and brightly colored birds. Regular walkers scatter handfuls of oatmeal, seeds, or peanuts for the sparrows and the squirrels. If the animals don't provide enough distraction for your stroll, there are plenty of wildflowers along the trail, shaded by a vast array of trees.

Even dandelions are objects of wonder to a toddler.

Try this hike at least once. You won't regret it. And you'll probably be back—again and again and again.

Getting There Glendoveer Golf Course is bounded on the north by Northeast Halsey Street and on the south by Northeast Glisan. It lies between Northeast 131st and 148th Avenues. To reach the start of the exercise path that circles the public golf course, take Halsey Street to 148th Avenue and go south on 148th. Turn right off 148th immediately afterward, and pull into the visitors' parking area for the Glendoveer Fitness Course. Tri-Met Bus 24 stops nearby.

It's also possible to join the Glendoveer exercise path from Glisan Street. There's access to the path on the east side of the clubhouse, just past the Ringside Restaurant. However, the parking lot on this side is reserved for golfers and restaurant patrons. You'll have to find street parking nearby. Tri-Met Bus 25 runs along Glisan, and there's a stop in front of the clubhouse.

Getting Around The Glendoveer exercise route is marked with mileage posts for travel in a counterclockwise direction. We've written up this walk to match the norm, but feel free to switch directions after your first visit. There's a pretty even mix of "clockers" and "counterclockers" among the course's regular walkers.

From the parking area on Halsey and 148th, angle slightly right to gain the sawdust-covered path along the golf course perimeter. Note the 2-mile marker as you begin. Watch for an Oregon white oak to the right of the trail just after you start out. There used to be a wooden identification sign near the trunk. Many of the trees in the first ½ mile of the course were labeled in the past, but vandals have stripped the fitness course of much of its "portable" charm in recent years.

Thimbleberry bushes and Oregon grape cover the ground beneath oak and maple trees as you continue. If you're walking in May, watch for the delicate white blossoms of miner's lettuce beside the trail. Flowering Pacific dogwoods add their glowing contributions to the color scheme in early spring.

Pass a Portugal laurel on the right, then a hawthorn tree. (It's covered with white blooms in spring.) You'll see more flowering dogwoods tucked in beside large Douglas firs. Just before the ¼-mile mark, watch for a group of four trees on the left.

The first two are California redwoods. The world's tallest known tree is a 368-foot redwood. These Glendoveer specimens should have plenty of time to grow, as redwoods are 400 to 500 years old before they reach maturity. The next tree in line is a western hemlock. Its droopy top is a trademark of the species. And the final tree is a deodar cedar. Its Hindu name means "timber of the gods."

The Glendoveer Fitness Course is "squirrel heaven."

Continue on level terrain, with views across Glendoveer's busy fairways. Watch for a trio of beautiful Colorado blue spruce in the grass. The steady drone of Halsey's traffic will accompany you as you walk. Note the perfectly shaped giant sequoia at the ½-mile mark. This tree is a member of the redwood family. Squirrels love its cones.

Reach the first corner, and veer left to follow the path along a row of houses. You'll enjoy respite from traffic noise as you walk past several tidy backyards. Hemlocks and Douglas firs offer their shade as you continue. Just after the ¾-mile mark, several warning signs caution walkers to watch for flying golf balls. If someone hollers "fore," cover your head and duck! Two errant drives landed on the path in front of us on our most recent visit to the fitness course.

Stay with the main trail as you wind into the heart of the golf course. A net-enclosed driving range is on the left. A tangle of footpaths winds beneath thick Douglas firs. Follow the flow of walkers, and stay on the main sawdust path.

You'll gain asphalt as you leave the driving range. Climb a gentle incline toward Glisan Street. Skirt the edge of the clubhouse parking lot, then veer left onto the sidewalk paralleling the busy thoroughfare. Glisan's traffic noise is an unpleasant backdrop to this section of the walk.

Walk to the far end of the parking lot, then reenter the golf course proper through an opening in the chain-link fence. You'll be accosted by squadrons

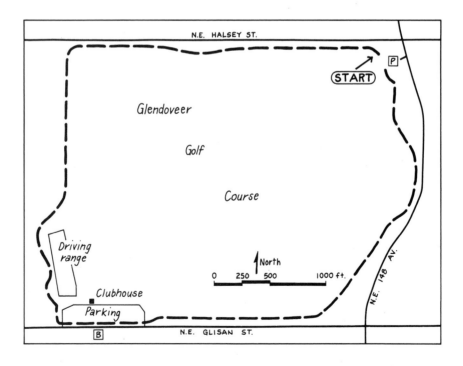

of shameless beggar squirrels as you wander through a tiny forest of Douglas firs. Stay on the sawdust path as you pass a silver water tank, then angle left with the pathway to leave Glisan Street behind.

The forested section that follows is the nicest part of the fitness course. Traffic noise is softer, although it's still audible. Bigleaf maples paint the forest orange and yellow in the autumn months, and vine maples and red alders add their brushstrokes to the canvas. In winter, English holly boasts red berries to brighten the walk. And the forest floor is green with ferns and moss.

Watch for gay white trilliums in March and April. The yellow flowers of Oregon grape are present, too. Of course, Glendoveer's squirrels are at their begging stations all year long.

Wind your way through the forest, and enter a more open area as you parallel 148th Avenue. Descend slightly and veer left with the path. Gain thick forest once again as you coast downhill beneath Douglas firs and bigleaf maples. The forest floor is green with sword ferns and Oregon grape. And red elderberry bushes compete with red huckleberries for the middle ground.

Emerge at the walkers' parking lot, and pause to catch your breath. Many of Glendoveer's walkers just keep right on going at this point. You'll get dizzy watching them. So why not join the flow and go around again?

Southeast Portland and Environs

◆ 16 ◆
Laurelhurst Park

Distance: 1⅓ miles (round trip)
Estimated time required: 30 minutes
Highlights: Great family park; children love the duck pond
Terrain: Level asphalt paths; accessible to wheelchairs and strollers
Best time to go: Loveliest in May, when rhododendrons are in bloom

Background In 1909, the 25+ acres of Laurelhurst Park were purchased for $92,000 from the estate of William S. Ladd (twice mayor of Portland and developer of Ladd's Addition). In 1910, under the masterful hand of John Olmsted (designer of the 1905 Lewis and Clark Exposition grounds and step-son of Frederick Olmsted, creator of New York's Central Park), a transformation was begun.

Over a period of several years, this swamp-bottomed parcel of land in southeast Portland was molded into the tree-shaded park that city residents know and love today. Laurelhurst Park has been a favorite of Portlanders for more than half a century.

Nestled between busy Southeast 39th Avenue and the handsome old

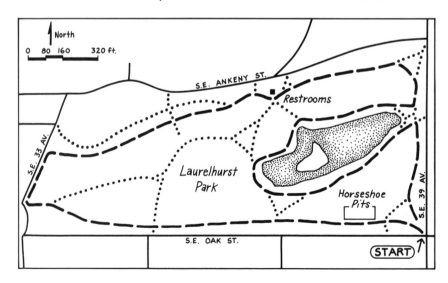

Labels on trees and shrubs make a walk in Laurelhurst Park a learning experience.

houses of the Laurelhurst residential district, Laurelhurst Park is one of Portland's hidden gems. It's popular with neighborhood walkers and joggers all year long, and it's lively with picnics, barbecues, and volleyball matches in the summer months.

For peaceful solitary walking, the morning hours are the best time for a visit. Unescorted women should not walk in the park after dark or very early in the day, as there have been scattered incidents of theft and molestation in recent years. Laurelhurst Park offers restroom facilities and drinking fountains.

This walk is excellent for those with strollers and wheelchairs, as the paths within the park are paved and mostly level. Unfortunately, careless cyclists sometimes make the asphalt hazardous for joggers and pedestrians, so always keep an eye out for speeding bicycles.

Getting There Laurelhurst Park is accessible via Tri-Met Bus 75, running on Southeast 39th Avenue, or via Bus 20 along Burnside. Burnside, Stark, and 39th are the major streets along the park boundaries. If you're arriving by automobile, parking is available on the residential streets to the north, west, and south.

Tree-lined paths and blossoming bushes await the visitor to Laurelhurst Park.

Getting Around Begin your walk at the corner of Southeast 39th Avenue and Southeast Oak Street. Tri-Met Bus 75 stops nearby, and there's parking available on Oak. There's a small recreation area between Oak and Stark that holds restrooms, drinking fountains, picnic tables, and tennis courts. From the corner of 39th and Oak, enter the park on an asphalt path and begin walking in a clockwise direction. Douglas firs will offer you their shade as you begin.

Continue straight along the south edge of the park and pass a large horseshoes competition area. On weekends, you might get a chance to watch a few of Laurelhurst's overalled veterans tossing ringers in a local tournament. Rhododendrons and azaleas line the pathway on the left (their colors are dazzling when the blooms are at their peak in April and May), and four tall California redwoods stand above them.

Laurelhurst Park is blessed with an abundance of tree and shrub species, many of which are labeled. Be sure to take the time to scan the names—at least on your first trip around the park. You'll find western red cedars, redwoods, giant sequoias, oaks, maples, and Douglas firs, as well as dozens of others.

Stay on the main trail as a footpath joins from Oak. Several more California redwoods line the way as you continue west. Reach another trail junction, and continue straight. To the right (just past the junction), a pair of giant sequoias spread their limbs. The path is level and smooth as you wander past an area of grassy picnic spots dotted with cherry and fir trees. On the left side of the path, London planetrees shade the way.

Pass a junction and a path coming in from Southeast 35th Avenue, and climb gently for a time. If you're walking in the morning or late afternoon, the sunlight slanting through the trees is almost magical. Continue straight past a turnoff to the right, and descend toward the western boundary of the park (33rd Avenue).

Turn right along the edge of the grass, noting a small dedication plaque at the base of a rough-barked oak tree. The plaque, commemorating the 200th anniversary of George Washington's birthday, is shaded by a handsome oak planted in 1932. One wonders why the group responsible didn't plant a cherry tree. Apparently, someone in authority gave the idea the ax.

There's a wheelchair ramp where the asphalt path leaves the park. (A driveway farther up the block provides access to another asphalt path.) You'll gain a break from the pavement for a while by walking about 200 feet north on 33rd and diving back into the trees on a pathway flanked by two Douglas firs. Notice how mercilessly the poor old fellows have been hacked to keep them from dropping rotten limbs on passing pedestrians. Pause to admire the striking cone-shaped silhouette of a more fortunate giant sequoia to the right before you continue.

You'll enjoy the natural bounce of the unpaved path as you walk beneath fir trees and drooping pines. Colorful rhododendrons and azaleas provide a lovely contrast to the rough-barked Douglas firs, painting a picture that's classic Oregon. Watch for a spreading horsechestnut tree on the hillside to the left (it blooms in late April), and listen for the chatter of birds in the stillness.

Pass hollies and magnolias before you cross a brick stairway and continue straight, merging with the northern asphalt track (wheelchair route). Note the impressive giant sequoia just off the pathway to the right. Follow the path toward the east. The small building on the left has restrooms. Veer softly to the left at the next junction (there's a drinking fountain here), and stay along the north edge of the park.

You'll begin to hear the unpleasant rumble of 39th Avenue as you stroll through a picnicker's paradise of grass, wooden tables, and scattered trees. Turn right at the junction on the east end of the park and parallel 39th as you walk south.

Turn right again to approach Laurelhurst's noisy duck pond, and stroll the asphalt path along the north edge of the water. Listen to the raucous honks and quacks of rowdy waterfowl as you skirt the perimeter of the pond. Laurelhurst Park's geese and ducks are almost always overfed, but they're never very sociable. Instead of talking with their human visitors, they prefer to gather on the small island in the middle of the pond, quack and honk, and generally raise a ruckus.

You can walk beside the pond on a gravel path at the water's edge, watching for the hungry catfish that hover near the shore, or stick to the asphalt route above. Swing left when the lake curves in, and cut across a stretch of gravel. (Wheelchairs should stay on the asphalt, as it's rough going here.) Scan the logs floating on the pond's dark surface as you walk. You might spot a group of resident turtles basking in the sun.

Regain the asphalt path and continue to circle the water, keeping to the left on the lower route as you stroll the south shore of the pond. Large trees line the way and the distinctive smell of the murky water competes with the aroma of pine needles in the air.

Continue in the direction of 39th Avenue as another path joins you from the right. At the far end of the pond, swing right up a slight incline to parallel 39th again. Dozens of Douglas firs shade the path. Pass a trio of thin European white birches, their white bark glowing in the shadows. And watch delightedly as bold squirrels dash up and down the tree trunks, ignoring the traffic and pedestrians as they forage in the grass.

Swing left at the next junction to reach 39th Avenue and regain your starting point. Or walk the loop again if you're looking for more exercise. If you'd like to mix this park hike with some pleasant urban walking, strike out into the surrounding Laurelhurst neighborhood and admire the vast lawns and spacious houses that make the area so picturesque.

◆ 17 ◆
Mount Tabor Park

Distance: 2 miles (round trip)
Estimated time required: 1 hour
Highlights: City and mountain views are fabulous on a clear day
Terrain: Steep hills and dirt paths; but paved roads allow wheelchairs and strollers
Best time to go: Avoid the crowds with a weekday or early morning visit

Background Mount Tabor rises 600 feet above the surrounding houses and businesses of southeast Portland, its gentle green bulge a familiar landmark to city residents. Named for Mount Tabor in Biblical Palestine, Portland's Mount Tabor was christened in the 1850s by Plympton Kelly, an early settler

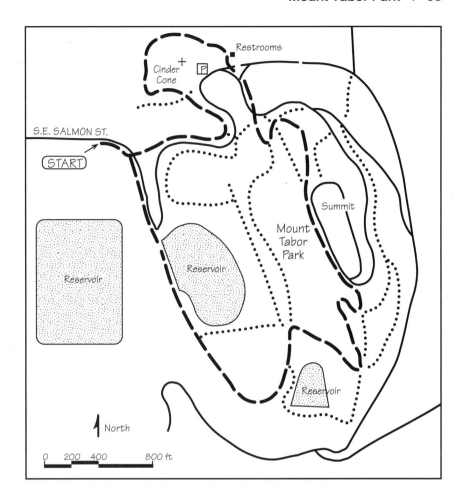

who homesteaded on nearby Kelly Butte. The mound has lent its name to the surrounding neighborhood, an area of large old homes and expensive newer dwellings.

Mount Tabor Park offers wonderful opportunities for pleasant hiking, with the added appeal of spectacular views available from its summit. Children will love this walk, as there's much to see along the way. If you're taking a dog along, keep it on a leash. The park is popular with neighborhood dog owners, and your pet is sure to meet a good number of unfamiliar canines on your visit. (Currently, there is an off-leash area in Mount Tabor Park where exuberant dogs do run free.)

Mount Tabor Park contains four large reservoirs that hold the city drinking water piped in from Bull Run (as well as several resident flocks of ducks). Bull Run water first filled Mount Tabor reservoirs in 1894. The reservoirs' handsome stone walls and sturdy iron fences are certainly worthy of attention. But the truly unique thing about Mount Tabor Park is a feature many visitors completely overlook—a volcano within city limits. And that once-fiery volcano is the now placid, tree-covered Mount Tabor.

Getting There Approach Mount Tabor from its western side, following Southeast 60th Avenue. The park is bounded on the south by Southeast Division Street and on the north by Southeast Yamhill. Tri-Met Bus 71 stops at the corner of Southeast Salmon Street and 60th Avenue. If you're driving, turn east off 60th onto Salmon Street. There is limited curbside parking before you enter the park proper. (If you can't find a parking spot, drive into the park and leave your car at the lot beside the volcano crater.)

Getting Around Climb gently on the sidewalk along Salmon Street and enter Mount Tabor Park. Because of repeated problems with nocturnal rowdiness, motor vehicles are prohibited beyond the park entrance between 8 P.M. and 5 A.M. Pass the swinging metal gate that helps enforce this regulation, and begin climbing along the road. Traffic can be fierce on a sunny weekend afternoon, so use caution as you walk.

If you have a stroller or wheelchair, keep to the asphalt road that climbs to the summit of Mount Tabor. You can veer off onto a carless road at the upper reservoir, and the walking improves considerably after that. We'll describe the trail route to the summit for hikers who want to escape both the traffic and the asphalt.

Continue uphill on the road, watching for the lower reservoir (the park's largest) on the right. You'll be surrounded by tall Douglas firs as you climb. Veer left onto a sawdust-covered trail that leaves the road just opposite the foundation of a long-destroyed stone shelter. Ascend steadily with the path as it winds past Douglas firs and rhododendrons. Sword ferns and English ivy cover the steeply sloping forest floor.

This trail can be muddy at times, so walk carefully. If you're hiking in the spring, the perky white blossoms of northern inside-out flowers will bob on skinny stems beside you, and pink-rimmed fringe cups will catch your eye, clinging to their upright spires. Red huckleberry bushes grow along the trail, as well, catching bits of sunlight with their leaves.

Mount Tabor Park is popular with Portland's high-school set, and you'll have to endure the revving engines and loud radios of hot rods going up and down the hill on sunny weekend afternoons. Unfortunately, you never really escape the presence of the cars (sight and sound), even on the trail. But it's nice to be out of reach of their tires for awhile.

Reach a junction in the trail, and veer left to avoid the steep pitch up toward the road. Skirt to the left along the hillside, climbing gradually in the shade of Douglas firs. You may be breathing heavily by now, but don't worry, the air you're sucking in will be sweet with the smell of damp earth and verdant greenery.

The candy-striped blossoms of Siberian lettuce are a sweet spring treat.

Continue to the left, merging with a second footpath. You'll have a nice view back along the hillside you've just negotiated. This section of the walk is especially lovely in late afternoon. The sun's rays sift through the branches of the firs, dropping golden ropes down to the forest floor.

Stay to the left as you continue climbing gradually. You'll be walking just below the asphalt road. Go straight on the main pathway, then cross a small road that descends steeply down the hillside. Skirt beside a chain-link fence and descend slightly, continuing through trees as you circle around the hill. There's a pleasant view down the slope to the left.

Stay with the trail and skirt around the hillside toward the north. Scattered trees allow an open vista to the west. If you're carrying a camera, you'll get a fine shot of downtown Portland from here. Continue your curving circuit on the hillside, hiking along Mount Tabor's northern flank. Enjoy a lofty look at the residential district just below. If the day is clear, you'll spot Mount St. Helens to the north. Look for the elusive form of Mount Rainier, peeking above the haze behind it. Share the way with squirrels, joggers, and walkers as you continue on.

Wildflowers are abundant here in the spring. Watch for the fluffy blossoms of false Solomon's seal, bobbing on long stems. Fringe cups and Siberian lettuce add their flowers to the color scheme, and the wide blossoms of thimbleberries brighten the forest gloom in May and June. Reach a chain-link fence that marks the boundary of Mount Tabor's volcanic crater. Climb gradually to a row of European white birches, and veer off onto the asphalt path to the right to walk down into the crater viewing area. A small amphitheater offers grassy lawns and wooden benches for picnickers.

Walk to the far end of the amphitheater to get a look at the old volcanic cinder cone. On the road above (near the basketball courts), there's an informational marker installed by the Geological Society of Oregon. Geologists believe that Mount Tabor was the scene of a tremendous explosion long ago—an explosion that filled the skies above present-day Portland with a fireworks extravaganza to shame any Fourth of July spectacular the city has ever known.

Experts claim Mount Tabor's eruption took place even before Oregon's volcanic Mount Hood was born (and long before Washington's Mount St. Helens stole the show). Today, the blackened rocks of the cinder cone sit atop Mount Tabor, as cold and lifeless as the burned-out wick of a birthday candle.

Retrace your steps to the trail at the northeast corner of the amphitheater and continue walking, skirting the left side of a small storage building. You'll hear the clamor of the large parking area as you go. Pass along the right side of a restroom facility, walking by large rhododendrons and scattered Oregon grape bushes as you follow the asphalt footpath.

Cross one paved road, then walk uphill along the shoulder of a second road. (This is the park's main thoroughfare, so walk facing traffic.) Stay on

A family takes a break from hiking to admire a fuzzy caterpillar.

this road for about 100 yards, then cross carefully and turn off onto the first trail to the right as the road curves to the left. You'll pass a large Douglas fir while climbing gradually. Come to another paved road (not for cars—just cyclists, skateboarders, and walkers), and turn left to follow it toward the summit.

After about 75 yards, turn right onto an unpaved footpath (just beyond an asphalt trail that takes off to the right), and climb steeply to the ridge-top. Walk south along the ridge, aiming for the small brick building just ahead. Mount Tabor's rollerbladers and skateboarders gather here on summer days, pausing to strap on elbow pads and summon their courage for the head-long journey down the hill.

Continue past the building, grab a cool drink at the water fountain, then cross the road and scramble up the grassy bank that rules the summit. Find a spot with your favorite view—west for the city proper or east for a glowing vista of Mount Hood. Spread out a blanket. Pull out a loaf of bread. Catch your breath and savor Mount Tabor's timeless treasures.

To begin your return to your starting point, regain the road and continue south along the ridge. There's a spectacular view of Mount Hood from the feet of a statuesque Harvey W. Scott, one of Portland's early civic leaders. Continue along the asphalt road to the middle of a U-shaped curve, then descend a set of concrete steps and gain a wide gravel path leading downhill through the trees.

You'll reach a four-way junction soon afterward. Take the branch to the right and descend along the hillside. False Solomon's seal droops with pink-ish berries in July. Zig to the left with the trail, and continue descending through the trees. You'll have a view of two of Tabor's reservoirs below. Sword ferns, English holly, and red huckleberry bushes line the trail. And bigleaf maples and red alders drop their shade onto the hill.

You'll appreciate the absence of traffic noise on this secluded section of the walk. Reach a lightpole, and veer to the right to gain a wide gravel trail. Continue descending past a sprinkling of hawthorn trees, then gain the as-phalt road again.

There's a drinking fountain just across the pavement. Look to the right down the hillside; you'll see Mount Tabor's soapbox-derby track. The wind-ing roads that climb Mount Tabor are often the scene of bicycle races, too. Go left on the asphalt road and continue your descent. (This road is closed to vehicles, so your vigilance needn't extend beyond cyclists, rollerbladers, and skateboarders.)

Curve around the south side of the hill, following the road until you're heading north again. You'll come in beside the large upper reservoir. Above it on the hillside, picnickers and sunbathers spread out in the grass on sum-mer afternoons.

If you want to lengthen your walk, stroll the loop around the upper res-ervoir (⅖ mile) or around the lower one (½ mile). The reservoirs' dark wrought-iron fences and old stone pump stations help give Mount Tabor Park its unique character.

Cross the metal barricade at the far end of the upper reservoir and rejoin the park's main road. Continue your descent along the shoulder to regain the park entrance, your car, or the 60th Avenue bus stop. If you'd like to blend a pleasant neighborhood jaunt with your park walk, the surrounding Mount Tabor residential district offers scores of lovely homes and many quiet streets for strolling.

◆ 18 ◆
Powell Butte Nature Park

Distance: 2½ miles (round trip)
Estimated time required: 1½ hours
Highlights: Fine view of Washington peaks from peaceful hilltop setting; neat forest stroll
Terrain: Mostly unpaved paths; limited access for wheelchairs and strollers
Best time to go: The view is lovely on a hazeless day; plan a sunny picnic, too

Background Powell Butte is a 570-acre volcanic mound in southeast Portland. Over the past decade, the city of Portland Park Bureau has been working hard to make Powell Butte Nature Park one of the city's premier recreation areas. Hiking, cycling, and equestrian trails have been constructed, mapped, and signposted. Picnic areas and restrooms have been put in, and links to Portland's 40-Mile Loop have been planned and implemented. With all this activity, the word is out, and Powell Butte is no longer the serene and often-overlooked hilltop it once was.

Visitors arrive by the carload here, especially on weekend days. As a result, problems with vandalism and litter, and conflicts between different types of trail users constitute just a few of Powell Butte's "growing pains." But the Park Bureau is committed to making Powell Butte Nature Park a true gem in the necklace of parks worn by the city. So go. Explore. And enjoy the "toddlerhood" of a truly remarkable urban wilderness.

Getting There Located between Southeast Powell Boulevard and Southeast Foster Road, Powell Butte claims a hefty chunk of southeast Portland between 145th and 174th Avenues. To reach the park, turn south off Powell at the lighted intersection with Southeast 162nd Avenue. You'll pass an entry gate and climb steeply on the paved road into Powell Butte Nature Park. (Please note that park hours vary by season. The gate is locked promptly at closing time—so don't be late!)

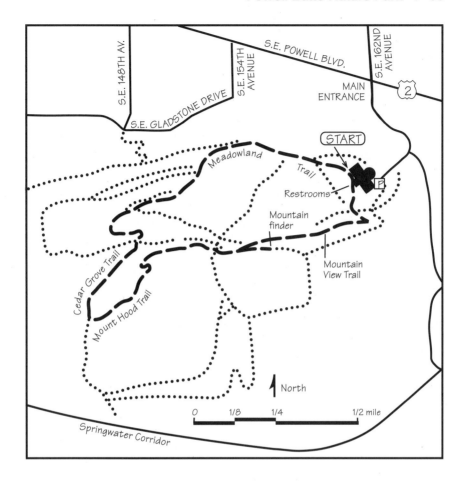

Leave your car in the gravel parking area at road's end. There are restrooms, picnic tables, and a drinking fountain here.

If you're coming by bus, Tri-Met Bus 9 runs on Powell Boulevard. Ask the driver for the stop nearest the park entrance, and hike uphill to reach the trailhead.

Getting Around Pause at the signboards by the parking area to gather information about the nature park. There's a free map dispenser (often empty) as well as a mounted map (currently inaccurate) of trails within the park's environs. Please remember that dogs must be leashed at Powell Butte. This is especially important, as horseback-riding visitors are frequent. The park is also home to more than 100 species of birds, as well as scores of rabbits and an occasional deer.

Set out from the west end of the picnic area with the paved trail. Walk a short distance and negotiate a U-turn toward the east. Just afterward, veer right to head uphill on a dirt track. You'll climb steadily past meadow grasses. The route is colorful with wildflowers in the spring. The white faces of wild carrots dot the hillsides later in the summer. And butterflies negotiate the hilltop breezes to flutter from blossom to blossom.

Ascend to a four-way junction, and continue with the trail straight ahead (Meadowland Trail). You'll pass an orange fire hydrant soon after. Enjoy level walking on the wide gravel route, and look for vistas of Mount St. Helens to the north. Stay with the path straight ahead as you pace onward, keeping the concrete drainage ditch on your left.

The songs of birds and the conversations of a million crickets intermix with the hum of traffic from Powell Boulevard. Pause to look behind you, and you'll be treated to a picture-perfect view of Mount Hood, framed above the green lushness of the meadow. Scraggly wild hawthorn trees accompany you as you press on. Then more trees join in from the right, clawing up the hillside with fingers of dark shade.

Douglas firs and bigleaf maples stretch skyward above tangles of sweet Himalayan blackberries. If you're hiking in August, you may be tempted to stop and sample. Be careful where you're picking, though. Powell Butte has one abundant hazard—poison oak.

Poison oak is a bushy plant with dark green, shiny leaves. The oval-shaped leaves have three lobes, or leaflets, and they're somewhat similar in appearance to oak leaves. The leaves, stems, and roots of poison oak deposit a troublesome oil on anything they touch. If you're sensitive to poison oak, you'll have itching and blistered sores within a couple of days after contact. Be sure to wash thoroughly with soap and water if you think you've touched poison oak. Although this won't eliminate the results of your encounter, it will help reduce the consequences.

Stay with the wide gravel route, skirting along the edge of the hillside. Watch for hoofprints in the dust as you continue. (And dodge anything else the horses might have left behind!) Curve left and climb gently to another junction. You'll cross the concrete culvert. Choose the left trail out of the trio of unpaved routes fanning out ahead.

Climb past more hawthorns. They're decorated with red berries in late summer. And use all your willpower to resist the aroma of the sweet blackberries that line the way. After about five minutes of walking (more, if your T-shirt now has blackberry stains), the route curves east, and you'll pick up the companionship of Mount Hood.

Start downhill, then take a small side trail after about 30 yards. You'll veer right to enter a fragrant, shadowy forest of western red cedar, vine maple, red alder, and tall Douglas fir. Sword ferns and bracken ferns duel for sunlight on the forest floor, and wildflowers are abundant in the spring. Fringe

Wonderful vistas and varied vegetation characterize Powell Butte Nature Park.

cups bob on long stems, and the five-petaled blossoms of Siberian lettuce dot the ground with spots of white. Yellow buttercups and false Solomon's seal add their gay blossoms to the springtime festivities along the trail.

Descend in the shadow of bigleaf maples and Douglas firs as you keep to the left past a handful of unmarked (and often confusing) junctions. If you do happen to lose your way in here, simply angle up the hill. You'll regain open ground (and your bearings) when you near the summit.

The descent through the forest is gentle at first, then the dive downhill picks up intensity. Watch out for encroaching stinging nettles as you walk. Reach the bottom of a small ravine where use trails fan out like the spokes of a wheel. Speaking of wheels, we encountered half a dozen young cyclists here on our last visit, many of them riding much too quickly. Be alert—and be ready to bail!

Cross the little creek at the bottom of the ravine, and angle to the right. Keep the water on your right as you descend more gradually past regal western red cedars and stately Douglas firs. If you have children along, watch for

The Port Orford cedar is recognizable by its rounded, reddish-brown cones.

a hefty western red cedar at the water's edge. Make the short detour to investigate its base, and your kids can stand "inside" a tree for a photo.

Cross another tiny creek bed and veer left just afterward to climb with the Mount Hood Trail. Endure a steady uphill push through the trees, then emerge onto Powell Butte's meadow-topped crown. Continue uphill to reach the old orchard area atop the butte.

If you're looking for a pretty picnic spot, this may be the place. You'll have a fine view, plenty of sun, and pleasant grassy surroundings. Apple, walnut, and pear trees clutter the summit, and the sweet scent of wild roses wafts on the breeze.

Continue east to the small viewing area ("Mountain finder" on the map) where the mountains and bluffs visible from Powell Butte are signposted. To the east, you'll see the mountains from which are cut the walls of the Columbia Gorge. And in the distance, a snow-covered Mount Hood floats on the horizon, catching the caresses of the sun. If the day is unusually clear, you might spot the tip of Mount Jefferson to the southeast.

It's possible to see four Cascade peaks from this spot on Powell Butte (St. Helens, Adams, Hood, and Jefferson). To the north, you'll see the spewing smokestacks of Camas, Washington, across the Columbia River.

When you're ready to leave the view at last, backtrack to the paved Mountain View Trail, and descend to the parking area and your starting point.

◆ 19 ◆
Oxbow Regional Park

Distance: 2⅛ miles (round trip)
Estimated time required: 1 hour
Highlights: Old-growth forest of Douglas fir and western red cedar; peaceful trails awash in wildflowers
Terrain: Moderate hills and unpaved trails; no strollers or wheelchairs
Best time to go: Try a weekday if you can; spring and fall are always lovely here

Background Located 20 miles from downtown Portland, Oxbow Regional Park is a 100-acre treasure, nestled into a looping bend in the Sandy River. Administered by the Multnomah County Parks Services Division, the park offers several miles of hiking trails, a lovely beach, and scores of picnicking and camping sites. Fishermen, boaters, and birdwatchers find plenty to entertain them here. And for walkers, Oxbow Park is "love at first hike."

Oxbow Park is an official part of the Oregon Scenic Rivers Program. The land shelters more than 200 varieties of native plants, 88 species of birds, 38 species of mammals, and 15 species of reptiles and amphibians. Deer, coyotes, raccoons, opossums, and porcupines inhabit Oxbow's forest; and owls, great blue herons, grouse, and kingfishers prowl its shores and skyline. Park regulations exclude dogs and alcohol, and there's a small entrance fee for cars entering the park boundaries.

You can visit Oxbow Park between 6:30 A.M. (7 A.M. in winter) and dusk, seven days a week. Wear boots or sturdy tennis shoes for your walk, and pack a lunch to eat beside the river. You'll receive a map of the park and its trails when you pay the entrance fee.

Getting There   To reach Oxbow Regional Park, drive east on Southeast Division Street. Beyond Gresham and Powell Valley, Division Street becomes Oxbow Drive. Follow signs for Oxbow Park, and turn left at the intersection with Hosner Road to gain Oxbow Parkway. Drive downhill on Oxbow Parkway to reach the river level and the entrance to the park.

Ask for the free trail map of Oxbow Park when you pause to pay your entrance fee, and be sure to take a look at your odometer. The trailhead for this walk is 1.4 miles from the entry booth, on the right side of the road. (It's marked on the park map by Junction D, just past the pump house.)

By the way, it is possible to enter Oxbow Park on foot and avoid the entrance fee. You'll have a 700-foot descent to the river level (and a 700-foot climb back to your car) if you continue straight onto Homan Road rather than turning left onto Oxbow Parkway at the final intersection before the park. Leave from the equestrian unloading area at the end of Homan Road, and descend to Junction G (see accompanying map) to join the described route.

There is no Tri-Met bus service to Oxbow Park.

Getting Around   Park your car at the pulloff beside Junction D (just past the pump house). A boulder-mounted plaque beside the trail proclaims this to be the "Pauline Anderson Forest." There's a drinking fountain here, as well. Leave the parking area on a narrow footpath, and continue straight at the first junction.

This first section of the walk winds through an old-growth forest of enormous Douglas firs and shaggy-barked western red cedars. Western hemlocks and bigleaf maples are well represented, too.

Stay with the shaded trail beneath the trees, gazing from side to side in admiration as you walk. If you're visiting in the spring, you'll find your attention divided between the trees and the abundant wildflowers. Watch for the tiny white blossoms of Siberian lettuce in April and May. The shaggy flowers of Pacific waterleaf are present, too, but they're not nearly as attractive; they have long purple stamens and greenish-white petals.

Angle left at the next junction, and pause to admire the massive Douglas fir on the left side of the trail. Catch the perfumelike fragrance of false Solomon's seal in April. The white blossoms cling to long, bending stems. Ferns are also abundant along the path. Sword ferns, lady ferns, bracken ferns, and maidenhair ferns will clamor for your attention.

Keep right at the next junction, then go left immediately after. Trilliums decorate this portion of the trail in March and April. In June, the almost microscopic blossoms of false mitrewort cling to delicate green stems, and pretty pairs of pink twin flowers hang like tiny bells, ringing brightly in the forest gloom.

Reach another junction and go right, passing beside an aged cedar as you begin a gentle climb. Keep an eye on the trailside vegetation as you proceed. Trios of cloverlike green leaflets mark the presence of wood sorrel. These little wildflowers boast pale pink blossoms in the spring, but their leaves are the most noteworthy things about them. They're edible—and actually quite tasty.

Another leaf you'll find quite interesting along this portion of the trail is that of the pathfinder plant, a unique wildflower with unimpressive blossoms riding atop skinny stems. The triangular leaves of this plant measure from 4 to 6 inches across, and their pale white undersides contrast sharply with the green upper surfaces. Turn a pathfinder leaf upside down as you pass. You'll leave a white arrow as witness of your trailblazing.

Climb to a junction marked with a wooden signpost labeled "E," and go right to continue up the hill. Gay Siberian lettuce and the dusty pink blossoms of wild bleeding hearts bring the trail to life in May. And moss-draped trees and berry-laden red elderberry bushes line the path, offering cool bits of shade. Listen to the whistles of the birds as you puff steadily uphill.

Ascend a steep grade toward the summit of the hill. This trail sustained

A pathfinder plant nestles in a bed of wood sorrel at Oxbow Regional Park.

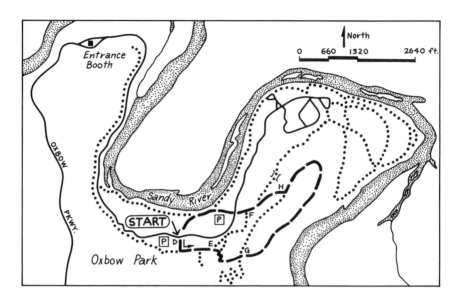

substantial damage a few winters past, but don't let a bit of downfall and some rough going deter you. You'll arrive panting at a four-way junction guarded by red alders. To the right, a trail comes in from the equestrian unloading area on Homan Road (alternate entry route).

Continue straight to walk along Oxbow Park's Alder Ridge. Signpost G is on the right side of your trail. The terrain levels out as you continue, but the quality (and aroma) of the trail may change with the addition of the horse traffic from Homan Road. Be sure to watch where you're going—or you may put your foot in it! Western hemlocks and bigleaf maples join red alders to offer you their shade. And wild bleeding hearts hang valentines between the ferns in spring.

If you're walking in September or October, you'll have plenty of color on this walk. The leaves of the maples and alders are ablaze with gold and crimson in the fall, and red elderberry bushes add their bright berries to the color scheme. English holly bushes decorate the trail with Christmas shades of green and red in the winter months. And the rainbow starts again in spring, with white-faced trilliums hiding in the ferns and bright green needles strung like lace on western hemlocks and Douglas firs.

You'll spy the glitter of the Sandy River as you near the far edge of the bluff. Continue through an open area of thin red alders. Rotting, fern-draped stumps are the handiwork of long-gone logging crews. Watch for a small foot-path shooting off to the right as you continue, and make the short side trip to a viewpoint on the edge of the bluff. Here you'll have a lofty vantage point above the twisting Sandy River. Don't get too close to the edge. It's a long way to the bottom.

Return to the main trail and continue walking. Stinging nettles are thick along the path. The five-petaled white blossoms of windflowers are a much more welcome presence in the spring. Oregon grape is abundant, too; you'll see dark "grapes" among the shiny leaves in summer. Arrive at a second footpath leading to another vista of the river. You'll have a fine view up the Sandy from here.

Continue along the plateau. Red alders and western red cedars shade scores of ancient fir stumps. After about 1½ miles, begin your descent to the river on a rough footpath churned up by the horses. At the junction marked by Signpost H, go right to descend more steeply toward the water on a wide, rocky trail. You'll know you're entering black cottonwood territory as you inhale the balsam fragrance of the trees. The path is carpeted with the white fuzz of the cottonwoods in June.

Continue straight past a trail descending to the right. Common horsetail lines the path as you near the water level. Cross the park road, and walk into the parking/picnic area just beyond. Work your way across the parking area, aiming for the covered picnic shelter straight ahead. Angle left at the wooden fence beyond the picnic shelter, and gain a trail above the water where the fence ends. (If you'd like to take a break beside the river, follow the footpath angling down to the water level from the right corner of the fence.)

Salal and red huckleberry bushes line the trail above the river. If you're walking in the summer months, the waterfront will be noisy with the shouts of sunbathers and boaters. The rest of the year, the Sandy flows in solitude. Keep to the main trail above the river, and angle left as you cross an access road. Stay on the main trail at the next junction, and walk beneath large Douglas firs and western red cedars. Fringe cups and vanilla leaf decorate the trail in spring.

Climb gently to a junction marked by a small stump and a boulder (on the left). Veer left here, and leave the river as you walk toward your car. Cross the park entrance road to gain the parking area and your starting point.

◆ 20 ◆
Oaks Bottom Wildlife Refuge

Distance: 2½ miles (round trip)
Estimated time required: 1 hour and 30 minutes
Highlights: Glimpses of great blue herons are a special treat; this wetlands walk is fascinating for a host of reasons
Terrain: Fairly level, but the trail is unpaved and rough; no wheelchairs or strollers
Best time to go: Try the morning hours to catch the early birds

Background Oaks Bottom Wildlife Refuge, officially dedicated as the city of Portland's first wildlife refuge in 1988, is a bird fancier's paradise. Widgeons, coots, mallards, pintails, kestrels, hawks, quail, and woodpeckers are just a

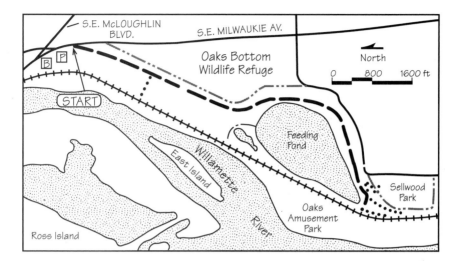

few of the birds a sharp-eyed hiker can spot on a walk through this 160-acre wetland. But the shining star of the Oaks Bottom show is a bird that even the casual observer can't ignore. With its 6-foot wingspan, its S-shaped neck, and its snapping bill, the great blue heron is hard to miss. And Oaks Bottom Wildlife Refuge is the favorite haunt of a score of great blue herons, the official bird of the city of Portland.

Oaks Bottom is a narrow flood plain on the east shore of the Willamette River. Bounded by a 100-foot bluff on the east and a railroad embankment that parallels the river on the west, the refuge is owned by the city of Portland and administered by the Parks Bureau. The Portland Audubon Society takes an active role in maintenance and planning for the refuge, too.

A trail built in the early 1970s by the Youth Conservation Corps provides access to the wetlands area. This is a wonderful hike for children, as the terrain is gentle and the distractions myriad. If you bring a dog along, be sure to keep it on a leash. Even the most well-behaved canine will have trouble resisting a splashing pursuit of the refuge's waterfowl. Wear sturdy shoes or boots for your visit, and carry a pair of binoculars.

If you like to explore, you'll probably be tempted by the many use trails that strike out into the wetlands from the main hiking route. Please be aware that the ground is fragile here. Wandering footsteps can destroy plant life very quickly.

Besides being important to the birds and animals that live here, wetlands such as Oaks Bottom have an extremely important role in maintaining the water quality of the Willamette River. They act as a filter for contaminants, a sort of natural "water treatment plant" to remove pollutants within the watershed. As such, wetlands like Oaks Bottom are worth protecting.

Enjoy your visit—but please treat Oaks Bottom with respect.

Attractions abound at Oaks Bottom Wildlife Refuge.

Getting There You can reach the trailhead for Oaks Bottom Wildlife Refuge from Southeast Milwaukie Avenue. There's a paved parking area on the west side of the road, at the intersection with Southeast Mitchell Street (immediately after you exit from southbound McLoughlin Boulevard). Tri-Met Bus 19 stops there, too.

Getting Around Leave from the south end of the parking lot, and pause at the informative signboard beside the trail to familiarize yourself with the refuge and its inhabitants. There are more than 140 species of birds represented at Oaks Bottom, and the refuge's variety of trees, shrubs, and wildflowers is enough to enthrall any budding botanist. The wetlands' heron population is at its greatest between February and June.

Continue walking past the signboard, and descend to the flood plain on the gravel trail. If you're hiking in August, the mouth-watering aroma of juicy Himalayan blackberries will sidetrack you immediately. Reach the level flood plain and continue south, skirting the base of the bluff. The main trail is about 4 feet wide. Be forewarned—it's flooded with mud in wet weather.

Keep to the main route, ignoring the offshoot trails that angle toward the river. Watch for pussy willows along the trail. They have wonderfully fuzzy "paws" in early March. Other trees along the bluff include swamp ashes, bigleaf maples, and black cottonwoods.

You'll lose the traffic noise from Milwaukie Avenue as you continue. The trail branches after about ⅓ mile. Veer to the left along the bluff. (The other trail provides access to the shore of the Willamette River.) Enter a wooded area of deciduous trees. It's rather barren in the winter months, but you'll have some nice views out across the refuge.

We spotted a group of 20 great blue herons circling above the feeding pond one day. One reason the herons are so numerous at Oaks Bottom is the refuge's proximity to Ross Island. This cottonwood-covered island is the home to one of the city's most active great blue heron rookeries.

In the spring and summer, the woods of Oaks Bottom are green with Himalayan blackberries, vine maples, and English ivy. Red alders, ashes, and black locusts are heavy with leaves, and a wall of cottonwoods obscures the view of the feeding pond. Autumn is a wondrous time along this trail. Whispering winds and fluttering leaves make the forest almost eerie, and the delicate orange blossoms of touch-me-not combine with the white fruit of snowberries to illuminate the path.

Cross a wooden bridge spanning a small creek, then continue on the gravel path. There's a wide, flat meadow on the right. It's sprinkled with black cottonwoods and Pacific willows. These water-loving willows boast wonderfully furrowed trunks and long leaves.

Perk up your ears and tune in your "built-in Walkman" as you hike. You'll hear the chirps of swallows, the caws of crows, and the quacking of mallards

A mother and son share the wonders of a quiet pond at Oaks Bottom Wildlife Refuge.

on the pond. Tree frogs are common in the wetlands, too. Listen for their "ribbits" as you hop along. The dull hum of traffic drifts into the refuge from across the river, reminding you you're on a city hike. And, if you walk the trail on a sunny summer afternoon, you'll have to endure the roar of boat engines, as well.

Continue along the hillside. In May and June, fringe cups bob along the trail, brightening the way with their pink-rimmed blossoms. Watch for a large Oregon white oak on the left side of the trail. If you're walking on a sunny afternoon, you'll see a steady stream of bees emerging from the openings in its sturdy trunk.

Pass beneath the imposing buildings of the Portland Memorial Funeral Home (there's a stately great blue heron painted on one wall), and climb gently to cross a second, much less sturdy wooden bridge. Red elderberry bushes and Himalayan blackberries crowd the trail in June, reaching out to grab at passing hikers. Views out across the feeding pond are wonderful from here. You'll marvel at the fluctuating water level as you visit during different times of year.

Late in the summer, look for the bright yellow faces of beggarticks blossoming beside the water. These wetlands-loving flowers are notorious seed spreaders. They "grab" passing hikers with sticky fingers and hitch a ride to fertile ground. The tenacity of beggarticks was noted by famed naturalist Henry David Thoreau in a treatise on the dispersion of seeds.

Arrive at a third footbridge, and continue to a white metal gate/barrier that spans the trail. The path branches just afterward. The route to the left ascends along the bluff, providing access to another entry point at Sellwood Park. Follow the trail to the right as it shoots out into the meadow.

Skirt the edge of the feeding pond, keeping an eye out for waterfowl along the shore. In February, you'll see patrolling pairs of mallards paddling the surface of the pond. They're paired for nesting, as are the great blue herons. If you're fortunate, you may get a look at the herons' courtship rituals. Bill snapping, neck stretching, plume fluffing, and noisy territorial disputes all come with the mating season. Be sure to give the nesting birds a wide berth, as they're disturbed quite easily.

The trail is level as you continue toward the river. The view toward the north takes in the high-rise buildings of downtown Portland. You'll see the rides at Oaks Amusement Park ahead of you as you walk onward. (Keep a tight rein on the children here!)

Climb a steep incline among grasping Himalayan blackberries to reach a set of railroad tracks. If you come in August, be sure to bring a bucket for the blackberries. Binoculars will come in handy, too. You can feast your eyes on the abundant bird life in the feeding pond while you sample the fruit on the surrounding bushes.

You'll probably be tempted to explore northward along the tracks from here, but several sternly worded warning signs should discourage you from tresspassing on the still-active rail line. If you're not crossing the tracks to visit Oaks Amusement Park, head for home by backtracking toward your starting point.

◆ 21 ◆
Reed College and Crystal Springs Rhododendron Garden

Distance: 2 miles (round trip)
Estimated time required: 1 hour (plus time for Crystal Springs Rhododendron Garden)
Highlights: Swampland wilderness at Reed College; cultivated elegance at Crystal Springs
Terrain: Reed College's rough trails rule out strollers or wheelchairs; Crystal Springs is perfect for both, however
Best time to go: Dry days are better for Reed College's pond; don't miss the April/May finery on display at Crystal Springs

Background This hike combines two markedly different walks—a swampland stomp through the wilds of Reed College's campus and a pleasant passage along the paved pathways of Crystal Springs Rhododendron Garden. The bulk of this walk's description covers the path through the Reed College campus, as Crystal Springs Rhododendron Garden is too civilized to need much explanation.

The campus path is very muddy in wet weather, so wear boots or old tennis shoes. If you're bringing children along, be sure to pack some cracked corn for the ducks. (Bread crusts aren't good for them and are notorious for gumming up waterways.)

Reed College was funded by the estate of Simeon Reed, a Portland businessman who earned a fortune in river commerce and real estate in the late 1800s. The school is more than 90 years old today, and the campus is snuggled into Portland's wealthy Eastmoreland neighborhood, surrounded by large homes and bordered by the emerald fairways of Eastmoreland Golf Course.

The sparkling waters of Crystal Springs Creek wind through the Reed campus on their way to Crystal Springs Lake in the heart of Crystal Springs Rhododendron Garden. A shaded footpath follows the water's route from the campus to the lake.

If you'd like to forego the wilderness sortie and spend your entire afternoon with the azaleas and rhododendrons at Crystal Springs, you'll find the garden at Southeast 28th Avenue and Woodstock Boulevard. It's open during daylight hours, seven days a week. (An admission is charged). Picnickers are welcome—and abundant.

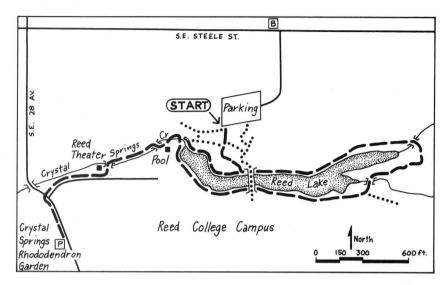

Getting There To begin your walk from the college campus, turn west off Southeast 39th Avenue onto Southeast Steele Street (or east onto Steele from Southeast 28th). Watch for a sign marking the entrance to "Reed College North Parking" on the south side of Steele. The lot is open to campus visitors. Tri-Met Bus 10 stops near the parking lot.

Getting Around From the parking lot, walk south onto the Reed campus, making your way past several small student dormitories. You'll soon spot the murky surface of Reed Lake just ahead. Descend toward the lake, veering left toward a large footbridge across the water. Just before you reach the bridge, turn right onto a steep trail and descend to the shoreline. Gain the footpath along the lake, and turn left, passing under the bridge as you parallel the shore in a clockwise direction.

Ducks are abundant in the small, shallow lake. Unlike their overfed neighbors in the nearby Rhododendron Garden, Reed's ducks are usually hungry. They'll paddle along the shore and keep you company, plying you for handouts while you hike. Pass the large pipe across the lake, and continue beside the water. Downed limbs and encroaching underbrush make the hiking adventurous, if not too rapid.

The hillside to the left has plantings of fir and Oregon grape. Fringe cups line the way in May, and bright orange California poppies brighten the hillside in June. Note the many red elderberry bushes, too. They're heavy with red berries in early summer (unless the birds get there before you do). If you do spot some berries, leave them for the birds—raw elderberry fruit causes diarrhea and vomiting in humans.

As you approach the swampy east end of the lake, watch for cattails in

Touch-me-not thrives in the damp soil near lakes and streams.

the shallow water. Stay with the path, and climb steeply up the hillside to leave the shoreline, passing a raised manhole cover on the right. Gain more level walking along the hillside. It's dotted with Himalayan blackberries and Oregon grape bushes. Bigleaf maples, red alders, and hawthorns catch the sun before it hits the ground.

Swing right and begin descending gradually to reach a large grassy area. Keep to the edge of the grass, then take the footpath to the right. Angle left along the hillside to reach the gully bottom. Continue to the right on the trail, merging with a lower trail as you walk toward the source of Crystal Springs Creek. One note of warning—the maze of use paths makes it easy to get confused in here—if you find yourself knee-deep in muck, you might want to do some backtracking.

The chirrups of birds and the chatter of squirrels playing in the trees provide a pleasant substitute for city traffic noise. The campus swamp is a popular recreation spot for neighborhood children intent on getting wet and muddy, so you'll probably have their shouts and splashes to keep you company, too.

Crystal Springs Creek bubbles from the swamp bottom beneath a canopy of red alder trees. If you visit in the early spring, watch for long yellow pollen clusters dangling from the branches of the alders. The clusters look like forgotten tinsel, hanging from a Christmas tree. It's easy to see how Crystal Springs Creek got its name. The water is as clear as glass as it emerges from the ground. If you're feeling tempted, don't drink. Despite the wilderness atmosphere, you're surrounded by the city here.

Turn south from the source of the creek, and continue on the footpath toward the southern shore of Reed Lake. Veer to the right at a junction where a secondary trail climbs to the campus lawns. Blackberry bushes are tangled across the hillside here. Several smaller trails turn off into the swamp bottom, but most of them end in ankle-deep mud. Stay on the main trail if you want dry socks.

Continue on level terrain, and gain the lakeshore once again. The muddiest parts of the trail have boards across them. They're still muddy, though, so walk carefully. If you watch closely, you may spot signs of the pond's resident beavers as you hike. Look for tooth marks on downed limbs and the brushy piles that mark small beaver lodges.

Pass the large pipe, and continue along Reed Lake's southern shore. You'll probably want to stay with the upper trail, as the footing is a little better. Warning signs prohibit swimming in or drinking from Reed Lake, but the mucky bottom is all the discouragement you'll need.

Pass under the footbridge, staying to the right with the path. The hillside is covered with English ivy, and Siberian lettuce challenges the overwhelming green with small white blossoms. In August and September, the tiny

Bright yellow skunk cabbage inhabits the muddy banks of Crystal Springs Creek.

orange blossoms of touch-me-not are abundant here. This beautiful little flower gets its name from its fragile fruit, which "explodes" when touched.

Be sure to keep an eye on the water as you continue. Great blue herons sometimes visit Reed Lake to rest and feed. They don't like company, and you'll probably get only a quick glimpse if you flush one out. Walk past a small wooden building on the shore, and continue to a hillside amphitheater.

Reach a campus maintenance parking lot, then go right to skirt the west end of the lake on a wide causeway. Veer sharply to the left on the other side, taking the lower trail beside the campus swimming pool (on the left). Spring daffodils dot the hillside on the right.

Stay along the chain-link fence at the far end of the pool, and descend beside Crystal Springs Creek. Cross the water on a small footbridge, and gain a wide path beside water. Swing to the left to cross another bridge, and continue on the south side of the creek. In April and May, the bright blossoms of yellow skunk cabbage infuse the creek bed with an odor in keeping with their name. Pause a moment to admire the "fragrant" blooms. (It's okay to hold your nose.) The flowers use flies as pollinators, attracting their airborne visitors with the aroma of squashed skunks. Animals eat the underground stems of the plant, and baked skunk cabbage was utilized by Northwest Indians as a winter diet supplement.

You'll climb the stairs of the Reed Theater (built on stilts above the creek) to leave the water level, and continue toward Crystal Springs Rhododendron Garden. Gain a campus service road, and turn right to reach Southeast 28th Avenue. Cross 28th Avenue carefully, and turn left along the sidewalk to walk toward the garden. Admire the beautifully shaped giant sequoia trees that line the path beside Eastmoreland Golf Course, forming a handsome fence with their massive reddish-brown trunks.

Reach Crystal Springs Rhododendron Garden soon afterward. There's a large parking area just off 28th, and you'll find a drinking fountain beside the entrance to the grounds. With more than 300 species of rhododendrons, a multitude of azaleas, and several colorful sprinklings of Pacific dogwoods, magnolias, and flowering cherries, this 7-acre garden is one of Portland's loveliest cultivated enclaves.

In 1988, Crystal Springs earned a mention in *Travel and Leisure* as one of the nation's finest gardens. Its fame is international, and you'll almost always encounter foreign visitors as you wander its asphalt lanes. The garden is at its most spectacular in April and May, but it's a lovely spot to linger in on any sunny afternoon. It offers grassy picnic areas, restroom facilities, and views of Crystal Springs Lake, Eastmoreland Golf Course, and Portland's west hills. The paved and gravel trails are excellent for wheelchairs and strollers, too. Weekends are incredibly busy at the garden, so try for a weekday visit if you get the opportunity.

To return to the Reed College campus and the north parking lot, retrace your steps to the college swimming pool and take the small dirt path along the north shore of the lake. Scramble up the bank above the footbridge to reach your car.

♦ 22 ♦
Tideman-Johnson Park

Distance: 1 mile (round trip)
Estimated time required: 40 minutes
Highlights: A corner of wilderness in the backyard of a city
Terrain: A mix of level asphalt and rough going; strollers and wheelchairs can be navigated only partway
Best time to go: Anytime you want to walk

Background Portland's Eastmoreland neighborhood is a captivating corner of the city. Developers laid out the area in the early decades of this century, and regal homes rule emerald lawns today. Throughout the neighborhood, curving avenues cut through quiet residential districts. But just below all the surface formality of Eastmoreland, a tiny park clings to its wilderness heritage, and rambunctious Johnson Creek rushes past its neighbors, hurrying toward its rendezvous with the Willamette.

A man named Tideman Johnson moved to this area in 1878, and he claimed a patch of land in the little canyon along Johnson Creek. His descendants deeded 6 acres of that claim to the city of Portland in 1942. Today that land has become Tideman-Johnson Park. Dive into this narrow wilderness along Johnson Creek, and you'll soon forget you're in the city.

Only the part of this walk along the abandoned rail line now known as the Springwater Corridor is suitable for wheelchairs or strollers, and unescorted women shouldn't venture into the lowlands along Johnson Creek at odd hours. If you have a dog along, please be sure to keep it on a leash. The creekside areas of Tideman-Johnson Park require very gentle treatment.

Getting There From downtown Portland, follow Southeast McLoughlin Boulevard south. Take the Tacoma Street East turnoff onto Southeast Tacoma, and cross McLoughlin on an overpass. Follow Tacoma to its intersection with Southeast Johnson Creek Boulevard. Go left on Johnson Creek Boulevard, and drive about a mile. Watch for a sign and paved parking for the Springwater Corridor Trailhead on the left.

The roomy lot offers restrooms, a drinking fountain, and picnic tables. It's a popular starting spot for cyclists setting out on the 16.8-mile Springwater Corridor, a paved trail built along an old rail line. This trail reaches all the

way to Boring at present. It's a part of Portland's 40-Mile Loop. (The name is deceiving—it's actually 140 miles.) It is hoped that the Springwater Corridor may provide a link to the Pacific Crest Trail through the Mount Hood National Forest in the future.

If you're using public transit to get to this hike, Tri-Met Bus 75 stops near the parking area.

Getting Around Walk to the west end of the parking lot, and head west on the wide asphalt trail. You'll want to use caution when you're on the Springwater Corridor route, as it's very popular with cyclists. Some travel slowly, some are on training wheels, but others are really flying—so beware! Thistles and Himalayan blackberries abound on the banks beside the trail, and tall black cottonwoods rustle overhead.

Look for signs for the 40-Mile Loop and the Springwater Corridor marking the route as you walk to a bridge above Johnson Creek. You can pause on the span to assess the mood of this rowdy waterway. It's famous for its high-water rampages in winter and spring.

Once across the bridge, swing to the left and coast downhill to enter Tideman-Johnson Park. If you're pushing a stroller, you'll probably have to turn back here, as the trails through the park are rough and unpaved. You'll enter a tree-sprinkled valley where Douglas firs, Oregon white oaks, and black cottonwoods drink from the waters of Johnson Creek.

Continue straight with the wide, unpaved trail to parallel the shore of this rambunctious waterway. Johnson Creek is several miles from its starting point near Troutdale as it rushes through Tideman-Johnson Park, but it has less than 10 miles left to go to reach its finish at the Willamette River.

Stay to the left with the path above the water. Scattered footpaths dive down to the water's edge. Unfortunately, many sections of the shoreline have been marred by careless footprints. Please respect this delicate habitat, and be careful where you walk. Sample sweet Himalayan blackberries in late summer, or marvel at the bigleaf maples in the fall.

The broad leaves of bigleaf maples are the largest in the maple family. They're particularly attractive in October, when crisp fall evenings turn them orange and red. Today, the wood of bigleaf maples is used for furniture and veneer manufacturing. But in the past, maple wood was a favorite with Northwest Indians. They used it to make paddles for their canoes.

Continue along the edge of the creek, pacing the unpaved footpath along the shore. Tall black cottonwoods make the valley fragrant with their distinctive scent, and open fields of grass invite picnics in the sun. This park is popular with a local crowd of dog walkers and baby haulers, but it's relatively unknown beyond the borders of the Eastmoreland neighborhood. If you come on a weekday, you'll probably have it to yourself.

The busy Springwater Corridor Trail passes above tiny Tideman-Johnson Park.

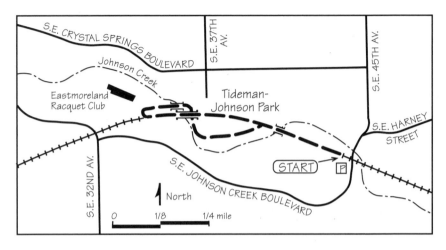

Walk to a pair of bridges spanning Johnson Creek. Go under the first, then veer left to take the lower bridge across the water. From here, a paved trail leads on past a blackberry thicket. You'll see the busy Springwater Corridor Trail above you on the left. Gaze at the sunlight on sword ferns and alder leaves as you pace onward.

Just before you reach the back lawns of the Eastmoreland Racquet Club, veer left to make the short, steep climb to the Springwater Corridor Trail atop the old rail bed. Thimbleberries and Himalayan blackberries crowd the shaded path as you ascend. You'll notice a major difference in the bushes right away. Thimbleberries don't have thorns; Himalayan blackberries have many. Keep your elbows in and soothe your scratches with a nibble while you walk. You'll find the thimbleberries ripe in early summer, but even then they're tart. The blackberries mature a little later in the season, and if their thorns are nasty, their dark seedy berries are oh-so-sweet.

Once you're up on the Springwater Corridor Trail (berry stains and all), go left from here to turn back toward the parking lot and your starting spot. You'll want to keep to the high route when a trail dives back down into Tideman-Johnson Park—unless, of course, you enjoyed the creekside jaunt so much you simply have to do it all again!

◆ 23 ◆
Elk Rock Island

Distance: 1 mile (round trip)
Estimated time required: 40 minutes
Highlights: Glimpses of nesting ducks and great blue herons in a wild river setting

Terrain: Rough and rocky trails with a lot of mud; no strollers or wheelchairs
Best time to go: Spring or summer weekdays for blossoms, birds, and solitude

Background If you're looking for a little-known corner of the Willamette waterfront, this walk on Elk Rock Island could be just the ticket. Because the island is secluded and largely undeveloped, this hike is definitely not for the timid. Don't be surprised if you have to step over the refuse of late-night drinking parties or if you stumble upon evidence of impromptu "campouts." Lone women would be better off leaving this walk for a day when they have hiking company. When you do make the journey to Elk Rock Island, bring a friend along, wear sturdy shoes, and carry a stick to knock away the spider webs.

Elk Rock Island offers no restrooms, drinking fountains, or formal parking lot, but its treasures are worth muddy tennis shoes and scratches from the blackberry bushes. Handsome native trees, delightful wildflowers, deep forest, and sandy beachline—what more could you want in a walk? Add in the ducks, rabbits, and great blue herons you'll see if you're observant, and Elk Rock Island is a picnic spread beside the river. All the island lacks is you. So come and feast your senses.

Getting There To find the trail to Elk Rock Island, drive south on Southeast McLoughlin Boulevard and take the turnoff onto Southeast River Road. Climb ¼ mile on the steep incline up River Road, then veer right onto Southeast Sparrow Street as River Road curves to the left. Go west on Sparrow to Southeast 19th Avenue. There's limited parking along the street. (There are also many "no parking" signs, so choose your spot carefully.)

Tri-Met Buses 33 and 34 run along River Road. You'll need to walk two blocks along Sparrow Street to reach the trailhead.

Getting Around Set out on the gravel footpath that leaves from the southern corner of the intersection of Sparrow and 19th. Scramble over a small mound, and walk between banks of Himalayan blackberries as you begin. Watch for the regal deodar cedar on the left side of the trail. Just in front of the larger tree, a skinny pussy willow is covered with furry "paws" in late winter and early spring.

The trail branches just beyond the pussy willow. Keep to the right, and descend toward the Willamette River on a dirt footpath. You'll pass several oneseed hawthorns on the right. These attractive trees are covered with delicate white blossoms in the spring. Oneseed hawthorns are natives of Great Britain, where they're used as living fences in place of stone or wire. They were imported to North America with early settlers 200 years ago, and they've become naturalized in the United States.

Traffic noise is minimal as you continue, and the melody of birdsong is a pleasant backdrop to your walk. If you're hoping for some glimpses of the

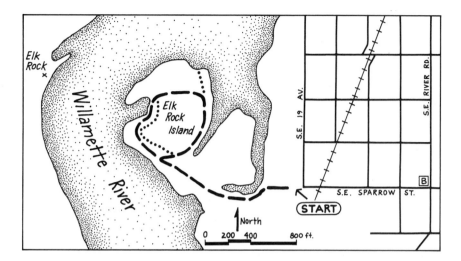

wild inhabitants of Elk Rock Island on your visit, try to walk as quietly as possible as you approach the river. Rabbits, lizards, and an occasional (harmless) snake will rustle in the underbrush as you walk by. Robins and sparrows flutter through the branches overhead. And ducks paddle on the pools along the riverbank or guard their hidden nests in spring.

Keep one eye on the sky, as well. More than 60 kinds of birds have been spotted here. Great blue herons are frequent visitors to the area. They feed on fish from the Willamette River and also eat lizards, salamanders, snakes, and dragonflies. It's always exciting to see one of these large birds lumber into flight.

You'll gain more level walking as you hike beneath tall red alders and even loftier black cottonwoods. Black cottonwoods are by far the most prevalent tree growing along Portland's varied waterways. Their fragrant leaves lend a special ambience to riverside romps. Common horsetail lines the trail here, its presence giving testimony to the moisture level in the soil. This section of the route is extremely muddy in wet weather, so watch your step.

Admire the yellow blossoms of a golden chain bush (flowering in spring) as you scramble up a short, steep hill, and continue on beneath an ancient-looking Douglas fir. Thimbleberries throw up a tangled wall of leaves and branches on the left. Stay to the left with the main trail, passing secondary footpaths leading to the water on the right. Then veer right toward Elk Rock Island as the main trail branches one more time.

Tall grass, pussy willows, and cottonwood trees line the way. Emerge onto a rocky shoreline, and walk straight across the promontory toward Elk Rock Island. If you're visiting when the river is high, you may have to utilize some fancy footwork to keep your tennies dry. Be careful on the rocks, as they're slippery when wet.

Shaggy-barked Pacific madrones are abundant on Elk Rock Island.

Ahead of you, you'll see the mound of Elk Rock Island springing from the river. Gaze at the outcropping of rock that rules the center of the island, and you'll get an overview of the tiny forest that awaits your feet. On the left end, Pacific madrones grow on curving reddish trunks. The trees are blossoming in early spring. To the right, Oregon white oaks lend their handsome profiles to the skyline. Straight-trunked Douglas firs hold the middle ground of the island, and more madrones and oaks take over at the northern end.

Gain a small dirt footpath on the far side of the rocks, and angle to the south side of the island as the trail curves to the left. You'll walk below several large Pacific madrones as you make your way around the island's perimeter. Catch the sweet fragrance of wild roses as you wander along the edge of a grassy meadow on the west side of the island.

You'll probably see some fishermen tending lines out in the river if you're walking in the spring. If you're hiking in July or August, you'll have to contend with the roar of powerboats, however. Those speedboats are the detriment of August hiking—the ripe Himalayan blackberries on the island are the benefit.

If you visit Elk Rock Island in June, watch for clumps of greenish-white flowers beside the trail, blossoming atop tall green stems. These pretty wildflowers are called hyacinth broadiaeas. They're members of a family of flowers known as fool's onions.

Gaze across the Willamette to the opposite shore. The sheer cliff face directly opposite Elk Rock Island is responsible for the island's unusual name. The cliff is known as Elk Rock. According to tradition, this bluff high above the river was a favorite gathering place for local Indians. Indian hunters chased wild animals off the cliff, sending them to their deaths on the rocks below. Afterward, the hunters climbed down to the bottom to retrieve their bounty.

When white settlers began arriving in the area, Elk Rock became the property of the Scottish grain merchant Peter Kerr. He began its transformation into a cultivated garden and cliff-top estate in the early decades of this century. It's now open to the public as Bishop's Close at Elk Rock on the west side of the Willamette.

Continue along the shoreline, and veer right toward the center of the island about 50 yards before you reach the rocky promontory topped by the green navigation marker (just opposite a tiny bay). If you have time for a small detour, continue out to the promontory and pause to read the small bronze marker on the rock. It commemorates the gift of Elk Rock Island to the city of Portland in 1940. Guess who the owner of the property was? The island's "upstairs neighbor," Peter Kerr!

Return along the beach, and turn inland to gain a dirt footpath that leads into the trees. One warning before you venture into Elk Rock Island's forest reaches—poison oak is well represented here, so don't venture off the trail. If you do happen to brush up against some poison oak while walking, be sure to wash off all the plant's oil as soon as possible. You'll probably want to launder your clothes and shoes, as well.

Enter the trees between Himalayan blackberry bushes that threaten to overwhelm the pathway. Scramble over a fallen log, and climb gently toward the center of the island. Fringe cups line the path in May, their cream-colored blossoms clinging to tall stems. You'll reach the top of a small rise and arrive at a three-way trail junction.

Turn left here, and pace onward in the forest gloom. On the right, a curious congregation of trees was planted in a tightly packed circle several years ago. The nine stout trunks huddle together like a football team preparing for a play. At their bases, fringe cups and trilliums compete with castoff garbage in the damp turf between their roots.

Walk beneath bigleaf maples as you continue past the team of trees. Wildflowers are abundant in the spring. Later on, you'll see the glowing white bundles that dangle from snowberry bushes in late summer. Reach a small clearing and take the path to the right on the other side. Thick growths of thimbleberries line the way. In April, May, and June, watch for the sweet-smelling blossoms of false Solomon's seal dancing above the ferns on slender stalks.

Climb gently as you walk beside Douglas firs dressed in tight overcoats of English ivy. Keep a sharp eye out for the beautiful purple blossoms of the tough-leaved iris. These lovely wildflowers blossom in April, May, and June. Native Americans gathered their fibrous leaves and wove them into ropes.

Stay on the main trail as you walk toward the south tip of the island, where Oregon white oaks spread their branches above Pacific madrone trees. Angle left with the footpath just before you begin your descent to the water. Note the initials etched into the twisted trunk of the large madrone on the point. Because of its soft wood, the madrone is a favorite canvas of romantically inclined carvers.

Follow the footpath gradually downhill to reach the water level, then turn left toward the east shore of the river once again. Retrace your steps to regain your starting point.

Southwest Portland and Environs

◆ 24 ◆
Marshall Park

Distance: 1 mile (round trip)
Estimated time required: 30 minutes
Highlights: A playful creek for summer-weary toes; a deep, dark forest for city-weary souls
Terrain: Moderate hills cut by unpaved trails; no strollers or wheelchairs
Best time to go: Choose a summer day for wading, or come in April for wild-flower watching

Background Marshall Park is one of southwest Portland's tree-covered treasures of undeveloped parkland. Hemmed in on every side by busy urban thoroughfares, Marshall Park lies undiscovered, glittering like a stolen emerald in the grasp of Southwest Barbur Boulevard, Southwest Boones Ferry Road, and Interstate 5. Come to Marshall Park on a rainless day and walk the trails beneath its trees. You'll find a wealth of wilderness, free for the taking.

The paths in Marshall Park can be rough and muddy, so you'll want to wear sturdy shoes and schedule your hike in dry weather. Bring along a picnic lunch if you have the time and inclination. Once you're immersed in this little forestland, you won't want to go back to the city.

Getting There To reach Marshall Park, drive south on Southwest Terwilliger Boulevard from Interstate 5. Branch to the right on Southwest Taylor's Ferry Road, and go left ⅘ of a mile later, turning onto Southwest 18th Place. (Note: There's a marked turnoff for Marshall Park on Southwest 12th Drive, but continue on to 18th Place to find our starting point.)

Drive south ⅕ of a mile on 18th Place. There's a small sign for Marshall Park on the left side of the road, just before a parking pullout. You can leave your car here while you walk.

Tri-Met Bus 43 runs along Southwest Taylor's Ferry, but you'll have to walk ¼ mile along 18th Place to reach the edge of Marshall Park.

Getting Around Enter the forest on the unpaved trail that descends beside the sign for Marshall Park. Angle right along the hillside, and veer sharply left at the first junction (just past the concrete posts) to continue steeply down the slope. You'll be immersed in the park's forest atmosphere immediately, as sword ferns gather on the ground beneath bigleaf maples and Douglas firs.

Arrive at a second junction and turn right, letting the pull of gravity drag your feet downhill. Maidenhair and bracken ferns join the ever-present sword ferns in their quest to subdue the forest floor, and yellow stream violets join the fray in springtime, tossing bombs of brightness onto an overwhelming field of green.

Watch for the white banners of trilliums if you're walking in March or April. Marshall Park has a legion of these early-blooming flowers. You'll see them everywhere along the trails. The trillium is also known as the "wake robin"—perhaps because it's the "early bird" of wildflowers.

Cross a small creek on a wooden footbridge. Stay to the right to walk beside the water at the junction just beyond. On some days, you'll have snatches of sunlight to warm you as you walk. And you'll share your way with parents keeping tabs on dripping children, as well as hikers, dog walkers, and perhaps a horseback rider or two. Watch for the thin white spires of vanilla leaf along the left side of the trail. The flowers bloom in April and early May.

Western red cedars and Douglas firs cast their shadows onto muddy patches of ground beside the water. Tiptoe through the muck as you follow the buttercup-lined trail, and arrive at the edge of an open, grassy picnic area (tables and play equipment here). Veer right to cross the feeder creek on one of two makeshift bridges, then go left to cross Tryon Creek on a wooden footbridge. You'll marvel at the fern-draped limbs of water-loving bigleaf maples as you continue.

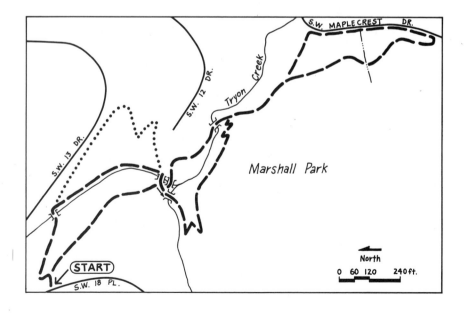

Climb beside the tumbling creek and let the chatter of the water fill your ears. You'll hear the squeals of children splashing in the pools if you're walking on a summer day. If your toes begin to murmur, promise them a dip when you're finished with your walk.

Continue your ascent beside the creek, then angle left to leave the water. Keep an eye out for stinging nettles along the trail. They're quite abundant in this section. Follow the winding pathway up the hill, and stay with the main route as you pass smaller trails heading into the underbrush. Watch for the

Northern inside-out flowers dance in the shadows in Marshall Park.

delicate blossoms of northern inside-out flowers in the spring. Each flower looks like a tiny white umbrella that has seen one too many windstorms.

Come in beside a chain-link fence as you hike above a steep drop to the water. Fringe cups and false Solomon's seal line the trail in May. In August and September, the white blossoms on the drooping Solomon's seal are replaced by bright red berries. Enjoy a zigzagging descent, and arrive at a junction beside the grassy field you passed on your way in. Go right and continue to a second junction. Take the upper trail as you angle to the right, passing between western red cedars on a well-worn path.

Cross a small creek running through a metal culvert, and continue on a pathway lined with trilliums. Watch for wild roses beside the trail just before you emerge on Southwest Maplecrest Drive. It's possible to cross Maplecrest and continue on the trail as it winds through the forest on the other side. Unfortunately, the pathway gets rougher and narrower the farther in you go.

To begin the return trip toward your starting point, turn left and walk downhill along the shoulder of Maplecrest Drive. Watch for a footpath diving into the trees from the west side of the road, just before you leave the boundary of the forest. Veer left to take the trail into the trees.

Vanilla leaf and fringe cups line the path as you climb beneath western red cedars and Douglas firs. Join the footpath you were on earlier, then go right at the next junction to stay beside Tryon Creek. Cross the water on an attractive stone bridge, and wander through a play area with swings and plenty of open lawn for picnics.

Angle toward the far upper corner of the grass and join a trail toward the creek. Go left to cross the water, then turn sharply to the right on a wide footpath. Keep to the left, then climb steadily on the wide main path. Walk beneath firs and cedars as you ascend toward 18th Place and your starting point.

◆ 25 ◆
Tryon Creek State Park

Distance: 2¼ miles (round trip)
Estimated time required: 1 hour and 30 minutes
Highlights: Wonderful forest setting in the heart of a big city
Terrain: Small rolling hills; some trails are accessible via wheelchair and stroller
Best time to go: The trilliums are wonderful in April; the trees are lovely in October

Background Thanks to the timely efforts of a citizens' group called Friends of Tryon Creek State Park, Portland is blessed with a 64-acre parcel of unspoiled forestland, just 6½ miles from the office buildings of downtown. The park we know today as Tryon Creek was on its way to becoming a housing development in 1969. But concerned tree lovers raised enough money to buy the land. The State of Oregon adopted it as a park. Volunteers built a trail system, and today Portland hikers have a quiet forest with more than 8 miles of walking trails to keep them happy.

Tryon Creek State Park occupies Tryon Creek Canyon, nestled between Southwest Terwilliger Boulevard and Southwest Boones Ferry Road. The canyon was logged in the 1880s by the Oregon Iron Company, and its trees provided fuel for Oregon's first iron smelter (Walk 26, George Rogers Park). Since then, the forest has recouped its losses with growths of Douglas fir, bigleaf maple, western red cedar, and red alder.

One of the special features of Tryon Creek State Park is the ⅓-mile paved Trillium Trail, completed in the fall of 1988. Built with donations and volunteer labor, Trillium Trail was the first handicapped-access trail in an Oregon state park. It is paved, flat, and accessible to individuals with limited mobility. And it winds through a lovely forest setting of Douglas firs, ferns, and wildflowers. In addition, Tryon Creek State Park has 3 miles of bicycle paths and 3½ miles of horse trails.

Getting There Reach Tryon Creek State Park from Southwest Terwilliger Boulevard, roughly 1 mile south of Lewis and Clark College. The turnoff is on the west side of Terwilliger, and you can leave your car in the large parking area just beyond the park entrance.

Tri-Met Bus 39 comes as close to the park as the intersection of Southwest Palater Road and Southwest Terwilliger, but you'll have a 1-mile walk to the Nature Center from there. (Use the bikeway that parallels Terwilliger.) Another option is to use Tri-Met Bus 38 along Southwest Boones Ferry Road, and access Tryon Creek State Park via the North Creek Trail.

Getting Around Head for the Nature Center (next to the parking lot) before you wander into the park proper. It's open seven days a week, and inside you can get a free park trail guide. Note the park regulations: stay on official trails, dogs must be kept on leashes, and don't pick the plants and flowers. The delicate white trilliums that serve as Tryon Creek State Park's unofficial emblem require seven years to reappear if plucked by overzealous admirers.

Park volunteers offer guided hikes on weekends and scattered weekdays. If you're interested, ask at the desk for a schedule. The Nature Center also boasts several fine exhibits on park vegetation, wildlife, and history, and there's a large relief map to help you get your bearings. We've written one suggested hiking loop for Tryon Creek State Park, but there are a host of other possibilities. Plan to spend several afternoons exploring.

Leave the Nature Center, and turn right at the signpost for the Trillium Trail. Leave the asphalt shortly afterward to continue straight on a wide bark-covered trail, following signs for Old Main Trail. You'll pass beneath thin red

Autumn leaves pad the pathways of Tryon Creek State Park in late September.

alder trees as you walk the level route. The area around the Nature Center is usually quite crowded, especially on weekend afternoons. But you'll gradually lose the people as you venture out into the park's more distant corners.

Reach another junction, and continue following signs for Old Main Trail. The Terwilliger traffic noise subsides as you walk on. The forest floor is covered with ferns. The shiny leaves of Oregon grape, Oregon's state flower, abound along the trail. The bushes are covered with bright yellow blossoms in the spring.

In addition to the clearly stated park regulations, you'll have another reminder to keep to the trails in Tryon Creek State Park. One brush with the numerous stinging nettles along the route and you'll lose all desire for trailblazing. If you're walking with children, be sure to warn them not to touch. The "sting" will last all afternoon.

Friendlier plants along the trail include a host of wildflowers. In May, Pacific waterleaf and fringe cups are abundant. The five-petaled white blossoms of Siberian lettuce are present well into the month of June. Salal and thimbleberry bushes are thick along the pathway, too.

Stay with the main path as you continue. After about ¼ mile, enter an area of ivy-covered Douglas firs. You'll feel like you're walking through a holly farm as you pass countless English holly trees. Their shiny, prickly leaves and bright red berries give a Christmas atmosphere to the forest floor.

Leave the Old Main Trail to veer left on the Red Fox Trail and walk steeply downhill. Pass several large western red cedar trees as you descend. The rough brown bark of the cedars looks like it's peeling right off the trunks. In fact, Native Americans of the Pacific Northwest region often stripped the bark from western red cedars. Bark strips were dried and beaten, then used for baskets, ropes, and mats.

At the bottom of the ravine, reach a wooden footbridge (Red Fox Bridge) spanning Tryon Creek. Climb steadily beyond the bridge, continuing straight at the junction to stay on Red Fox Trail. The forest in this section consists of many deciduous trees. The branches are bare in winter and early spring, allowing open vistas and the caress of sunlight on your shoulders as you walk.

Thirty yards past the junction, watch for a massive Douglas fir stump on the right side of the trail. It's a lovely, decaying sculpture—a piece of nature's

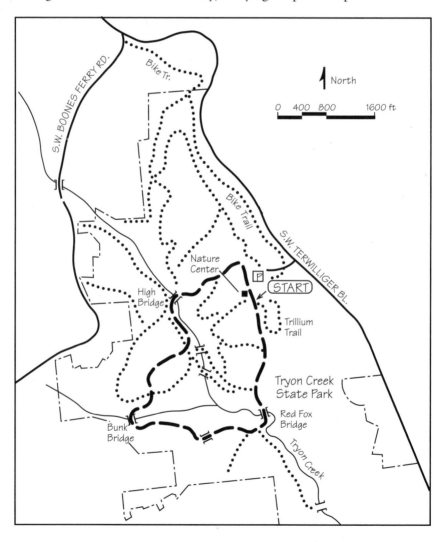

constantly changing art. The ferns that grow out of the top of the dead stump are witnesses to the ongoing life of the forest community.

Climb steadily on a rough dirt path. It's muddy in wet weather. Take a sharp right at the signpost, following a sign for the Cedar Trail. If you're in the mood for a short detour, take the small path to the left instead, and explore the little swampy area not far from the junction. Return to the Cedar route, and climb steadily to reach a ridgetop. You'll gain more level terrain on top.

Western hemlocks, bigleaf maples, and western red cedars overlook the path. If you're hiking in winter or early spring, you'll be able to see down into the Tryon Creek ravine as you continue. Note the long yellow pollen clusters hanging from the red alder trees.

Another benefit of springtime hiking is the presence of the trilliums. Tryon Creek State Park has an annual contest to see who can spot the first trillium of spring. The lovely white blossoms of this early-blooming plant have been found in the forest in late February some years. The "promptness" of the trillium is the reason for its other name—"wake-robin." The flower seems to bloom just as the robins awake in spring.

Descend into another small ravine, using caution on the muddy trail. Cross the creek on a small bridge, then climb steeply past scores of vine maples and holly trees. The trail levels out as you take a roller-coaster route along the ridge. Trilliums are abundant here. And the blossoms of Pacific waterleaf take over when the trilliums begin to fade.

You'll pass a small swampy area on the right. Watch for skunk cabbages in the water—or close your eyes and sniff for them. Reach a signpost and follow signs for the Cedar Trail, continuing straight ahead. There's a large laurel bush not long after the signpost. You'll know it by its shiny oblong leaves. In the city, these bushes are often used as hedges. Continue on in the shade of bigleaf maples, red alders, and western hemlocks.

As the trail angles sharply to the right, watch for several Douglas fir stumps towering above the ferns. If you look closely, you'll see deep grooves cut into their sides. These are springboard notches, cut by loggers more than 80 years ago. The men built wooden platforms around the trees so they could stand above the ground and wield their bulky saws. New trees have grown up to fill the sky, but these notched stumps are the loggers' footprints in the forest floor.

Descend again, and reach another footbridge (Bunk Bridge) across the creek. The creek bottom is thick with red huckleberry and salmonberry bushes. And a host of ferns give witness to the moist surroundings. Veer right as you leave the bridge, and climb steadily away from the water. Gain more gradual terrain as you hike beneath western red cedars and red alders.

Come to a four-way junction, and continue straight across the Horse Loop to stay on the Cedar Trail. Descend steeply into a thick forest where the tree trunks are covered with ivy. As you walk beside a small creek, you'll notice skunk cabbages in the water and more springboard notches in trees.

Cross the Horse Loop one more time, and continue straight, following the footstep signs. If you're interested in ferns, Tryon Creek provides an amazing variety of them. Sword ferns spring from the shaded soil beneath the Douglas firs. Maidenhair and lady ferns thrive around hidden springs. And wood ferns sprout from rotting stumps, transforming decay into a bouquet of living green.

Go left at the junction just beyond, and continue walking toward High Bridge. Late in the summer, the orange blossoms of touch-me-not dangle from thin stems. Watch for the large birdhouses in the trees as you walk beside the water. Despite the efforts of Friends of Tryon Creek, there is a housing development in this lovely wilderness—but at least it belongs to wood ducks and woodpeckers!

Stay on the main trail, and cross a swampy area on a plank walkway. If you have children along, you may want to wander down into the swamp and look for tracks along the water. We spotted muskrat footprints one afternoon. Some folks claim that a few elusive beavers inhabit the canyon, too.

Join the Horse Loop, and cross the creek on a wooden bridge (High Bridge). Reach a four-way junction and veer right toward the Nature Center, then finish off your hike with a final "puffer" as you climb steeply to the ridgetop.

The trail levels off and the population density increases as you approach the Nature Center. Keep to the left at the signed junction, stay on the main trail, and regain the park entrance and the parking lot. You may want to pause and study the trail map once more before you go—if you love this forest as much as we do, you'll already be planning your next hike here!

◆ 26 ◆
George Rogers Park

Distance: ¾ mile (round trip)
Estimated time required: 30 minutes
Highlights: Pleasant riverside stroll
Terrain: Paved, level path; excellent for wheelchairs and strollers
Best time to go: Nice all year

Background George Rogers Park hugs the west shore of the Willamette River, guarding the spot where Oswego Creek tumbles down the hill from Lake Oswego. Here the creek emerges from a narrow, rocky canyon, destined to lose itself in the river's ocean-bound flow.

The area of George Rogers Park was first settled around 1850, when New York immigrant Albert Alonzo Durham built a sawmill on the creek. The little waterway had been called Sucker Creek by early settlers, but Durham renamed

Wheelchair users find smooth and scenic travel on the trail at George Rogers Park.

it Oswego Creek after Oswego, New York. The area began to prosper when iron ore was discovered in the surrounding hills, and the first pig iron made west of the Rocky Mountains was produced here in 1867 by the Oregon Iron Company.

The remains of Oregon's first iron smelter can still be seen at the north corner of the riverside parking lot. There's an inscription at the base of the old brick structure that gives a brief history of the Oregon Iron Company. Oswego Creek supplied the water power for the smelter, oxen hauled in ore from Iron Mountain (west of Lake Oswego), and Douglas fir trees from Tryon Creek Canyon (see Walk 25) were utilized for charcoal.

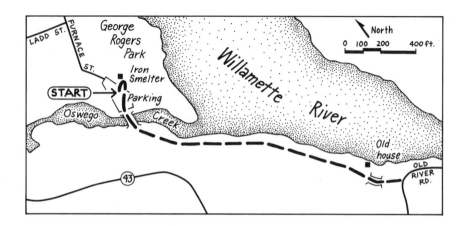

Named for George Rogers, a Lake Oswego grocer who took an active role in establishing the park, the area offers a ball field, tennis courts, a nifty playground, a picnic shelter, and river access. Today, the park is popular with families and picnickers. Fishermen patrol the banks of Oswego Creek, and some river visitors use the boat ramp to launch their powerboats. Best of all (from a walker's viewpoint), the park offers a pleasant riverside path that's perfect for strollers and wheelchairs.

Getting There George Rogers Park is accessible by Tri-Met Buses 35 and 36. Both stop on State Street. Walk along the park's north side (Ladd Street) to reach the river. If you're coming by car, turn east off State Street onto Ladd, then turn right on Furnace Street to reach the riverside parking lot. There are restrooms and a drinking fountain nearby.

Getting Around Make your first stop at the old iron smelter beside the parking lot. After you've paused to read the inscription, you may want to wander down to the shore for a close-up look at the river. The beach at George Rogers Park is packed on sunny weekend afternoons, and the roar of passing speedboats can be downright irritating. If you prefer more solitary strolling, visit the park in winter or on a drizzly day. Your dry feet will appreciate the park's paved pathway, and your soothed senses will enjoy the silence.

Walk to the southern corner of the parking lot to gain the riverside path, and cross Oswego Creek on a large footbridge. Just across the bridge, a dirt trail takes off into the canyon. If you'd like to add some rougher scrambling to your pavement pacing, you can join the fishermen along Oswego Creek and wander among boulders and ferns as you hike upstream. The trail fades out after about ¼ mile. The small concrete structure at the back of the canyon marks the site where electric power was first generated to light up Lake Oswego.

From the footbridge, continue straight to stay on the paved riverside trail.

Since this footpath connects with Old River Road at its southern end, it's a popular route with cyclists cruising along the river. Watch out for bike riders as you walk. If you have small children along, be sure to keep them within reach at all times. There are no barricades on the trail, and the riverbank is steep and high.

Walk along a hillside that's green with sword ferns and English ivy. Siberian lettuce is abundant in the spring, brightening the greenery with its delicate pinkish-white flowers. And red elderberry bushes add to the color scheme, dangling bright red berries above the path in the summer months.

Apartments and condominiums rule the ridgetop above the trail, but their presence goes unnoticed beside the charms of the Willamette River. Red alders and bigleaf maples line the riverbank as you continue. Listen for the calls of river birds as you walk.

Pass a tiny waterfall on the right side of the trail. Soon after, a sturdy footbridge replaces a washed-out section of the path. You'll reach a strange abandoned house after about ⅓ mile. Just before it, watch for a large Pacific madrone on the right. Pacific madrones are unique among Portland area trees. You'll recognize them by their peeling, reddish bark. The orange-red fruit of these trees was harvested by Native Americans, and the wood is sometimes utilized for weaving shuttles today.

Stroll onward past the mystery house sitting atop a concrete pier, rooted in the river. Continue walking to another footbridge. This marks the end of the official pedestrian route. You can keep hiking on paved Old River Road if you'd like to stretch your stroll a little farther. Traffic is fairly light on the quiet thoroughfare. Otherwise, retrace your steps to the parking lot to complete your hike.

◆ 27 ◆
Mary S. Young State Park

Distance: 2¼ miles (round trip)
Estimated time required: 1 hour and 20 minutes
Highlights: A pleasant stroll through a deep riverside forest
Terrain: Level hiking on sawdust-padded paths; no wheelchairs, strollers are okay
Best time to go: A weekday if you have one; or try a weekend morning in the spring

Background The land for Mary S. Young State Park was donated to the State of Oregon with the requirement that the acreage be maintained in its natural condition. That's not always an easy task, especially when large numbers of visitors present a need for parking lots, picnic shelters, and restroom facili-

Families love the forested trails of Mary S. Young State Park.

ties. Fortunately for forest-loving walkers, though, Mary S. Young has retained much of its wild personality. And the construction of perimeter and riverfront trails enables park visitors to explore the forest comfortably.

Mary S. Young is open from dawn to dusk, seven days a week. There are restroom facilities and drinking fountains available, as well as plenty of spots for picnicking. The trails are generally well maintained, although scattered rough spots may require sturdy walking shoes. Bring a friend and a yearning for the forest, and come to Mary S. Young to exercise your love for nature.

Getting There To reach the park, drive south from Lake Oswego on U.S. Highway 43 (continuation of Southwest Macadam Avenue and State Street).

Pass the grounds of Marylhurst College, and continue south to the park turnoff on the left side of the road, approximately 2¾ miles from downtown Lake Oswego.

Turn into the park proper, and continue on the entrance road to a large parking area near the river. Drive to the north end of the lot to park your car.

Tri-Met Bus 35 runs south from Lake Oswego on Highway 43. Ask the driver for the stop nearest the park entrance. You'll have to continue on foot to gain the starting point for this walk.

Getting Around Pause at the map for Mary S. Young State Park at the northeast corner of the parking lot. This will provide you with a good overall view of the area. You'll find an asphalt trail heading into the trees beside the map. Begin walking toward the river.

Oregon white oaks shade the path. You'll arrive at a junction immediately after you leave the parking lot. Angle left onto an asphalt trail. If you're walking on a weekday, you'll be immersed in quiet. Only the whistles of the birds disturb the silence here. Walk beneath a canopy of bigleaf maples as you cross an asphalt bike path, and continue straight onto an unpaved trail.

Angle left at the next junction. Red elderberry bushes line the way. They're heavy with red berries in the summer. Thimbleberries are abundant in the forest, too. You can sample the thimbleberries' fruit in July and August. Beneath the bushes, sword ferns and bracken ferns compete with English ivy for the forest floor. If you're walking in the early spring, you'll see many trilliums among the greenery.

A little later in the spring, watch for northern inside-out flowers dancing like dainty ballerinas on thin stems. False Solomon's seal makes the pathways fragrant with its sweet-scented white blossoms, and Pacific waterleaf parades its rather homely flowers through the wildflower beauty pageant.

Turn right at the next junction, staying with the sometimes-muddy trail. Watch for the thin white spires of vanilla leaf springing from the soil as you hike beneath Douglas firs and bigleaf maples. You'll marvel at the size of some of the maple trunks beside the trail.

If you're hiking with children, you might suggest a contest for finder of the biggest maple leaf. The leaves of the bigleaf (or "broadleaf") maple can reach a width of 10 inches!

Continue through a deep, dark section of the forest. Wildflowers huddle in the shade, hoping for unclaimed spots of sun. After about 10 minutes, descend steeply with the trail. Curve around a knotted old maple trunk, then climb steadily between red alders and vine maples.

Reach a four-way junction, and turn right to stay along the park's perimeter. You'll walk along a fern-filled ravine, then scramble down a steep incline to cross a tiny creek. Pause to admire an enormous Douglas fir as you head downhill. Sword ferns, maidenhair ferns, and lady ferns crowd along the banks, competing for every morsel of open ground available. Maidenhair ferns, in particular, love shade and plenty of moisture. You'll often find these delicate ferns wriggling their "toes" in muddy forest creeks.

Climb away from the water, walking beside a bank overrun with thimbleberries and salmonberries. Watch for a hefty Douglas fir on the left side of the trail, then pause to admire the massive stump in the forest to the right. Just beyond the stump, you'll see an old fir snag, riddled with the holes of woodpeckers. Continue straight at the next junction, staying on the unpaved trail.

Be careful not to brush your hands against the crowding stinging nettles that line the way. If you're walking in April or May, you'll see cream-colored fringe cups blossoming on upright stems. And Siberian lettuce and false Solomon's seal add to the spring array. Later in the summer, the delicate orange blossoms of touch-me-not bob on thin stems, dancing in the shadows.

You'll lose the dark shade of the fir trees for awhile as you walk beneath Oregon ash, bigleaf maples, and vine maples. This part of the forest is especially lovely in the fall, when the dying leaves are painted with a score of colors. Oregon white oaks add to the variety of the trees, as well. But keep an eye out for another "oak"—the troublesome poison oak plant is an unwelcome presence along this trail.

Stay on the main route as other pathways intersect from either side. If you're confused at the many junctions you encounter, don't worry. You've got a "natural" guide right at your feet. Look for a small green plant with triangular leaves. The pathfinder plant is a wonderful trail marker. Flip one of the leaves so that the light-colored underside is facing up. It works like a directional arrow to "point" you on your way.

Siberian lettuce and blue-pod lupine line the trail in May and June. And ferns are everywhere. Watch for bracken ferns growing on long stems. Bracken ferns are the tallest of the Northwest ferns, towering above their shorter cousins to get the first chance at the sun. Bracken ferns are quite resourceful, too,

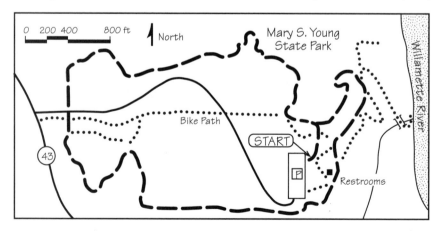

growing well in a wide range of moisture and light conditions.

You'll begin to hear the traffic noise from Highway 43 as you approach the west side of the perimeter trail. Cross the paved entrance road, and continue down the pathway on the other side. You'll come to the park's asphalt bikeway next. Cross it, too, and stay with the unpaved route as you walk.

About 20 yards beyond the bike path, watch for a group of corn lilies on the right side of the trail. These unusual plants grow to 8 feet tall, with long green leaves that start right at ground level. Their whitish-green blossoms cling to stout, leafy stems in May and June. These plants are extremely poisonous, causing birth defects in sheep, killing insects, and even doing in unsuspecting honeybees.

Continue to the right along the park's perimeter, then begin to lose the traffic noise as you angle in toward the river. You'll reach a junction marked by an old stone drinking fountain (not in use); go right on the perimeter trail. Walk beneath red alder trees, and watch for the blossoms of orange honeysuckle in the spring. Northern inside-out flowers, Siberian lettuce, yellow stream violets, and fringe cups are scattered in among the ferns.

You may be feeling hungry by this point in your walk. If you're hiking in August, help is near. Fat and juicy Himalayan blackberries thrive beside the trail, tempting you to pause and pick. Gather sweet fruit, a few scratches, and a T-shirt stain or two, then skirt the edge of an open field as you walk toward the parking lot. A wide variety of trees are planted in the grass.

Arrive at the south end of the parking area. Go left on the paved pathway, then turn right toward the river on an asphalt trail. You'll pass a long-dry drinking fountain and a shaded picnic area as you walk beneath oaks, red alders, and bigleaf maples. Curve left to parallel the parking lot, and continue with the asphalt trail to reach a paved service road. Go right to descend toward the river.

You'll reach a Y after a quick descent. If you'd like to get down to the shore of the Willamette and don't mind a bit more downhill (with the accompanying uphill, of course), you can take either branch from here. You'll have to scramble through some brush and high grass to reach the shore at last. Pause and enjoy the river ambience, then retrace your steps to the little wooden bridge near the Y junction.

Cross the chortling creek on the footbridge, and climb above a marsh on an often-slick plank walkway. You may be breathing hard as you ascend several sets of wooden steps. Common horsetail is abundant in the marsh, and you'll see the bright yellow blossoms of skunk cabbage as well.

Puff up the stairways, and continue up the hill on an unpaved footpath. Keep to the left as you top the rise, and walk beneath western hemlocks as you continue. Angle right at the next junction, then go left at an intersection guarded by a yellow fire hydrant.

Follow the trail back toward the parking lot. Hungry again? Head for the blackberries before you head for home!

◆ **28** ◆
Gabriel Park

Distance: 1½ miles (round trip)
Estimated time required: 40 minutes
Highlights: A pleasant mix of grassy park and hidden forestland
Terrain: Rough dirt and sawdust paths; no wheelchairs, strollers would
be tough
Best time to go: On the spur of any moment

Background Gabriel Park is one of Portland's many grassy treasures, snuggled
into a residential area of homes and schools and grocery stores. The park's
90-acre size allows energetic walkers a long perimeter stroll, and it holds a
hidden treat for forest lovers—two tree-shaded ravines, complete with trilliums, ferns, and Himalayan blackberries.

If you're bringing children along, plan to make this walk an all-afternoon
excursion. You can picnic in the sun, play on swings and slides, or fly a kite
above extensive lawns. There are restrooms and drinking fountains in the park,
and there's a bakery/deli on Southwest Vermont that will deliciously replace
all the calories you've worked off.

Getting There You can reach Gabriel Park on Tri-Met Bus 1. Ask the driver
for the stop on Southwest 45th Avenue, closest to the tennis courts. If you're
coming by car, swing south off Southwest Vermont Street (or north off Southwest Multnomah) onto Southwest 45th Avenue, and turn east off 45th into
the park proper. There's ample parking in the lot beside the tennis courts.

Getting Around Gabriel Park is big and open and uncomplicated, and you
can pretty much wander at will, even on your first visit. We've written up a
suggested walk to get you started, combining a simple stroll around the
park's perimeter with some exploratory hiking in two forested creek bot-
toms. The tree-shaded trails will be muddy in wet weather, so choose your
shoes accordingly.

From the parking lot, turn east and walk along the pathway between the
tennis courts. Stroll into the center of the park, following the roller-coaster
pathway through the grass. You'll pass between a Douglas fir on the right
and a bigleaf maple on the left as you continue. If you're guiding children on
this hike, spout some Oregon natural history to set the tone. Oregon's state
tree is the Douglas fir, named for the Scottish botanist David Douglas. It's
one of the most important timber sources in the United States, and it
provides forage for deer, elk, and grouse. And the bigleaf (or "Oregon") maple
was utilized by Northwest Indians to make canoe paddles. Today, it is much
loved for its brilliant foliage in the fall.

Climb steadily on the path, and arrive beside a row of young pine trees. You'll hear the murmur of the traffic as it drifts across the open fields from Vermont Street. Unfortunately, the skinny pines aren't thick enough to muffle the auto racket much. But you'll find some silence later on, as you dive into the forested recesses of the park. Share your way with dog owners, joggers, and neighborhood walkers as you continue.

Walk beside a line of tall Lombardy poplars as you approach Southwest 37th Avenue. A recently developed wetlands area invites gentle exploration, just south of the trees. It can also be accessed later in the hike, so you might want to save your detour for then.

Turn right on 37th, and walk along the edge of the grass. You'll cross over a small creek and arrive at Southwest Nevada Court. Sandwiched between two private driveways directly across the street, a small footpath/alleyway continues south. You have to look hard to find it. Follow the lead of neighborhood cyclists and shortcut strollers, and take the footpath to Southwest Caldew Street.

Turn right on Caldew, and descend past a mixture of older homes and newer suburban dwellings as you approach the eastern boundary of Gabriel Park. You'll find an unpaved trail into the trees awaiting you at the end of Caldew Street.

Reenter the park, and walk beneath a canopy of maple leaves. Oregon grape bushes line the trail on either side. Oregon grape is the state flower of Oregon, and it boasts bright yellow blossoms in the spring. If you're walking

A young couple enjoys a leisurely stroll beneath the trees in Gabriel Park.

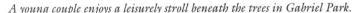

later in the year, you might spot berries on the shiny-leaved bushes. Oregon grape berries are edible—but one taste is usually sufficient!

If you're walking in the summer months, you'll breathe the scent of warm fir needles as you continue. Angle right past a twin-trunked western red cedar, then immerse yourself in a wonderful urban forestland. The songs of birds take over where the traffic noise leaves off. The air is cooled by the fanlike branches of countless Douglas firs. And the ground beneath your feet is cushioned with the cast-off needles of the trees. In the spring, wildflowers crowd the trail, brightening the forest floor with dots of white and yellow.

Look for northern inside-out flowers along the path in May. The delicate white blossoms are unmistakable. Watch for fringe cups, too. These flowers cling to long thin stems. And the rims of the white, cuplike blossoms are edged with pink, as if a woman wearing lipstick had sipped from every one of them. Sword ferns cover the forest floor with green, and trilliums hide among the ferns in March and April, turning their white faces toward the sun.

Cross tiny Vermont Creek on a wooden footbridge, and veer left as the trail branches. Continue beneath a gathering of western red cedars. The ground beneath the trees is almost devoid of underbrush, so complete is the cedars' monopoly of the sun. Descend to a muddy creek gully. The slopes are slick in wet weather, so watch your step. Cross a creek on a dilapidated wooden bridge, and watch for the massive western red cedar trunk at the far end.

Veer right on the footpath, and climb gently beside the creek to reach a Y junction. Continue to the left on the main trail as you gradually angle away from the water. This is a popular off-road riding spot for neighborhood cyclists, so you'll probably see lots of tire tracks in the mud.

Turn sharply to the left at the next junction, climbing steadily as you continue. Puff up a steep incline, and angle left with the trail just before you reach an open meadow. Western red cedars form a living curtain with their shaggy trunks as you walk along the north side of the field.

Keep to the footpath beside the field, ignoring the trails that dive left into the forest proper. Angle right and climb gently once again, and stay right to pass a handsome hawthorn tree and emerge into the field. Continue out into the meadow, following a worn footpath through the grass. Go left to skirt along the border of a farmer's field, bounded by a wooden fence. A tempting fruit orchard fills the area to the right.

Pass a sign for Gabriel Park Community Gardens, and continue to the left along a gravel entrance road. Swing right to gain a path toward one of the park's Little League baseball fields. Take a break at the drinking fountain, then skirt the third-base side of the baseball diamond. Watch for a European chestnut tree on the right side of the path. Unlike the much more common horsechestnut, European chestnuts provide an edible nut. Roasted chestnuts are beloved as an autumn treat in much of Europe.

Continue out into a long, grass-covered rectangle, paralleling 45th Avenue. There's a thin strip of forestland along the west side of the meadow.

And brilliant rhododendrons add their colors to the green of trees and grass in spring. Out on the lawn, fat-trunked maple trees spread their branches toward the sun, offering shady nooks for would-be picnickers.

If you're looking for a pretty spot to linger awhile, this is certainly the place to open a book or toss a Frisbee. Watch out for the line of western red cedars that rules the center of the meadow, though. These bushy trees are notorious kite eaters.

Amble downhill on the pathway through the grass to reach the far end of the meadow. When the trail angles left toward 45th Avenue, keep right to

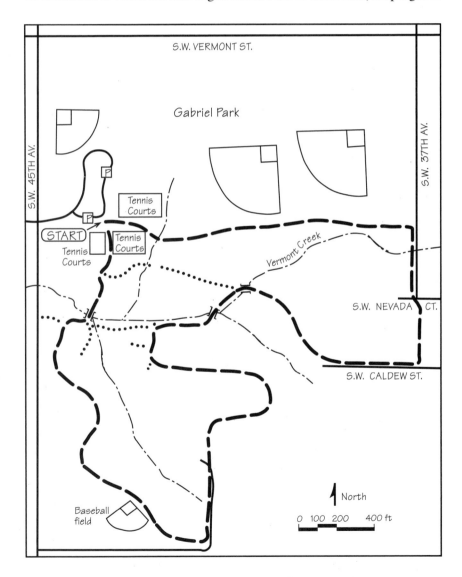

walk steeply downhill toward Vermont Creek. Cross the water on a wooden bridge, and climb gently through the grass beyond, aiming for the tennis courts and your starting point.

◆ 29 ◆
Woods Memorial Park

Distance: 1 mile (round trip)
Estimated time required: 30 minutes
Highlights: An unexpected forest hidden in the midst of a city
Terrain: Steep slopes on rough trails; but a paved road allows some wheel-chair and stroller use
Best time to go: Choose a dry day if you're venturing off the road; the blooms are best in April and May

Background Woods Memorial Park is yet another of Portland's untapped wells of wilderness, drilled deeply into the center of suburbia. In this tiny park, bounded by busy Southwest Taylor's Ferry Road and Capitol Highway, chortling Woods Creek winds through a tree-shaded ravine. Wildflowers play among ferns and fir trees, and rough trails descend the hillsides to end as muddy streamside pathways.

If you live within easy reach of this little forestland, don't let another weekend pass without scheduling a visit. And if you live on the other side of Portland, plan a walk in Woods Memorial Park the next time an errand takes

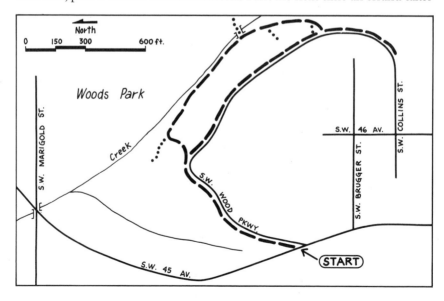

you to the neighborhood. Although it's small, undeveloped, and relatively unknown, this park is definitely worth exploring.

The paved (but carless) Southwest Wood Parkway passes through Woods Memorial Park on its winding route from Southwest 45th Avenue to Southwest Collins Street. You can push a stroller on this ½-mile ribbon of asphalt, or take a wheelchair down this silent, tree-lined corridor. You might see a local jogger or a couple of cyclists rolling down the pavement. But most of the time, you'll have the forest to yourself.

For the more adventurous visitor, we've written a walking route that mixes in some off-road stomping with the pavement pacing. Wear boots or sturdy tennies if you're going to use the trail—and plan to get a little bit muddy before you're done. This little pocket of forestland is woefully scarred by dozens of use trails, so it's difficult to describe an ideal hike (and perhaps even harder to follow the description). But give our route a try. If you don't cross the creek on the gully bottom and you remember to ascend the hillside to get out, you shouldn't get too lost anyway!

Getting There To find Woods Memorial Park, take Southwest Capitol Highway to Southwest Taylor's Ferry Road. Drive west on Taylor's Ferry to Southwest 45th Avenue. Go north on 45th, and turn right onto Southwest Wood Parkway after ¼ mile. There's room for a few cars at the west end of the road, just in front of the concrete barriers that exclude motorized traffic from Wood Parkway.

Tri-Met Bus 43 provides the best access to Woods Park. The bus line runs along Taylor's Ferry Road. Get off on 45th Avenue, and walk ¼ mile to reach Wood Parkway and the starting point for this hike.

Getting Around Enter Woods Memorial Park on Wood Parkway. If you're a fan of horsechestnut trees, you'll fall in love with this asphalt avenue right away. More than a dozen beautiful horsechestnuts spread their blossom-laden branches above the pavement. Plan to visit in May when the pink flowers are at their loveliest.

You'll see flowering wild cherry trees in Woods Park, too. There's a large specimen on the left side of the road, just after you enter from 45th Avenue. It's covered with brilliant white flowers in April and early May. The rest of the year, you'll recognize the wild cherry by the gooey rings around its trunk. The fruit of the wild cherry tree is popular with birds and small animals, but one taste will tell you why it's also called "bitter cherry."

Just beyond the bitter cherry, you'll pass two massive horsechestnut trees. Vine maples shade the road as you descend toward yet another horsechestnut. Veer left onto a small footpath as Wood Parkway curves to the right at a 90-degree angle (just beyond the horsechestnut).

Leave the asphalt and walk downhill on the path, angling left through a small, buttercup-sprinkled meadow. Continue steeply down the hill, with sword ferns pricking your ankles as you pass. Go right at a junction overlooked by rough-skinned Douglas firs. The murmur of the stream will draw you down the slope. Angle right soon afterward to descend gently along the hillside.

Cross a small creek as you continue toward the bottom of the little ravine. Fringe cups pour their pink-edged blossoms onto long thin stems in May. You'll see the shiny green leaves of Oregon grape bushes everywhere, and soft, damp moss covers the steep slopes, clinging to the soil with lime-green fingers.

Reach another junction and continue straight, angling along the hillside in a gentle descent toward the water. The pathway will deteriorate as you approach the bottom of the canyon. If you're walking in tennis shoes, you may get a little mud between your toes. Watch for the thick growths of common horsetail rearing skyward from the creekside muck. The familiar spiny stems of these moisture-loving reeds give testimony to the dampness of the soil.

The murmur of Woods Creek will drown out every sound of urban traffic as you walk beside the water. Step through the shadows of tall western red cedars as you continue. You'll pass the remnants of a rusted car body as you slog through a particularly muddy stretch of trail, then climb gently with the path. Just before the trail descends to cross the creek on a wooden plank, veer steeply up the hillside on a narrow footpath. Note the double-trunked western red cedar that marks the junction.

(If you'd like to explore farther along the creek bottom, you can cross the creek and continue on the path. Be very careful, though, as the rotting planks that served as a "bridge" on our last visit looked ready to collapse at any moment. And be forewarned, you'll only find dry walking here after several weeks of rainless weather.)

From the junction at the bottom of the ravine, climb steadily to another trail junction and angle to the left. Western red cedars and Douglas firs offer their shade as you continue up. Sword ferns cover the slope, and the white blossoms of thimbleberries add a touch of gaiety, like dancing whitecaps in a sea of green. Veer right at yet another junction in this maze of trails, and continue steadily uphill.

Watch for the delicate blossoms of Siberian lettuce as you walk. It's not hard to see how these tiny five-petaled flowers got their common name. Each white petal is streaked with peppermint-pink lines, making the perky "candyflowers" look good enough to eat. Yellow stream violets add their voices to the flowers' song in spring, and false Solomon's seal, Pacific waterleaf, and northern inside-out flowers join in.

Trilliums usually beat the other wildflowers to the punch. They're often dressed in their spring finery by March. Climb past another junction, and emerge onto paved Wood Parkway again. To extend the walk a bit, turn

Common horsetail rears skyward from the marshy ground in Woods Memorial Park.

left and follow the asphalt road to Southwest Collins Street. You can avoid retracing your steps by taking Collins west to Southwest 46th and turning right. Walk one block to Southwest Brugger Street, and turn left to reach Southwest 45th. It's a short walk back to the parking pulloff from there.

If you prefer the forest setting of Woods Memorial Park for the remainder of your walk, return on Wood Parkway and wander past more pink horsechestnuts as you gallop back toward your starting point.

◆ 30 ◆
Fanno Farm House and Greenway Park

Distance: 2½ miles (round trip)
Estimated time required: 1 hour
Highlights: A pleasant spot to stretch your legs on a lunch hour or after a shopping trip
Terrain: Level walking on paved pathways; ideal for strollers and wheelchairs
Best time to go: Whenever you feel like walking—an all-weather, all-year hike

Background Greenway Park and adjacent Fanno Farm House Park offer pleasant, easy walking in the midst of Tualatin's urban sprawl. Businesses and housing developments crouch around the edges of the narrow strip of green, but only joggers, pedestrians, cyclists, and rollerbladers venture in. The level terrain and paved pathways make this walk perfect for baby strollers and wheelchairs, and the mudless paths make wet-weather walking very comfortable.

On the edge of Greenway Park, a slice of local history is represented by Fanno Farm House. Built in 1859, Fanno Farm House is on the National Registry of Historic Places. Its proprietor, Augustus Fanno, gained fame and prosperity by developing and growing a breed of onions specially adapted to Oregon's damp climate. His prosperity allowed him to build the distinctive farmhouse. The Tualatin Hills Parks and Recreation District has restored the historic structure.

Getting There To reach Greenway Park, follow U.S. Highway 217 south from Beaverton, and take the Progress exit. Turn right onto Southwest Hall Boulevard. Drive northwest on Hall for ½ mile, and gain Greenway Park just before the intersection with Southwest Greenway.

This area is heavily developed, and there is no on-street parking on Hall Boulevard. Parking may be found along residential streets in the vicinity.

If you're coming by bus, Tri-Met Buses 76 and 78 run along Hall Boulevard. Get off at the intersection with Southwest Greenway, and walk to the northeast corner of the Albertson's parking lot to gain the paved trail entering the park.

Getting Around Greenway Park is an open, grassy rectangle surrounded by commercial and residential developments. It's virtually impossible to lose your way in the tidy little enclave. The park is long and skinny, and paved paths loop around its perimeter from one end to the other. Try our suggested walk on your first visit, then lengthen, shorten, or alter the route according to your personal preference.

This walk winds through both Greenway and Fanno Farm House Parks on the south side of Hall Boulevard, but it's also possible to explore the parkway on the north side of the busy thoroughfare. However, you'll need to return to the traffic light at the intersection of Greenway to be safe (and legal) when crossing Hall.

At the north corner of the Albertson's parking lot, gain the asphalt path and walk south into Greenway Park. Keep to the left as the path branches. Well-tended lawns may prove to be tempting for sunbathers and picnickers. Continue walking to a compact outdoor fitness course, and veer left at the junction to make the short detour to Fanno Farm House.

Enter a thin planting of Oregon ash and red alders, where sword ferns pierce the shadows with their pointed fronds. In April, May, and June, fringe cups blossom on their skinny stems, brightening the pathway with their flowers. Scattered hawthorns sparkle with red berries in the summer months.

Cross Fanno Creek on a wooden footbridge, and pause to search out Himalayan and trailing blackberries, oceanspray, and European bittersweet among the foliage. Fanno Creek, a 13-mile-long waterway that flows into the Tualatin River, is the heart of an important wetlands area. As such, it's home to a host of plant species and a great variety of animal and bird life.

Migratory birds pause here on journeys that encompass thousands of miles. Other birds, such as great blue herons, wood ducks, and red-tailed hawks, call this wetlands home. Not only are the wetlands an important wildlife habitat, they are an integral part of flood management in this watershed. You'll

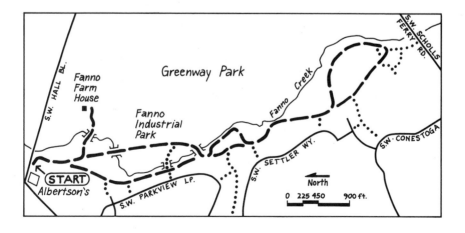

see the results of a decade of work toward restoration and preservation of Fanno Creek as you take this walk.

From the shaded bridge, climb gently toward the old farmhouse, strolling in the company of grizzled Oregon white oaks. Circle around to the front of the farmhouse on the asphalt trail. Upon first examination, it's difficult to get a feel for the history of Fanno Farm House. "Restoration" has meant new paint, a new roof, and a gleaming white picket fence for the little house. Even though the sign in front says the structure was erected in 1859, the house just looks too tidy to be that old.

Pause beneath the gnarled oaks behind the house, and admire the massive trunk and lovely silhouette of the tall black cottonwood in the farmhouse's front yard. Perhaps then you'll sense the passage of the years this place has seen.

Retrace your steps to the trail junction beside the fitness course, and turn left onto the main asphalt path. Watch for a handsome Oregon white oak off to the left, just before you cross the creek on a wooden bridge. Keep to the left as you continue. You'll share your way with a wide variety of walkers. There are arm-pumping exercisers, weaving "Sunday strollers," and older couples pacing arm-in-arm—in Greenway Park you'll seldom be alone.

The traffic noise from Hall Boulevard fades as you walk deeper into the park. To the left, the buildings of Fanno Industrial Park form the park's eastern boundary. Young bigleaf maples, hawthorns, and assorted evergreens are planted throughout the grounds. In another 30 years, the park will be much different.

Just before you reach a tennis practice wall and a small playground, veer left across the grass to study an informative signboard about the wetlands area. Peer into the skies above the marsh, and perhaps you'll spot one of the wetlands' winged creatures, sprung into life from the words on the board.

Return to the path and continue on, staying on the main pathway. Cross the creek again, and go left at the junction just beyond. Continue on level terrain as you walk toward Southwest Scholls Ferry Road. Go left again at the next junction. The creek will run beside you, its banks overrun with wild roses.

Cruise on between oak trees and Himalayan blackberries, and keep to the left at the next junction. Cross a small stream and stay left again. You'll pass a young giant sequoia standing in the grass. Although this fellow doesn't have the impressive height of older family members (giant sequoias can live to be 1,500 years old and grow as tall as 250 feet), you'll recognize him from his lancelike needles and reddish-brown trunk.

Enter a forested area where Oregon ash trees cast deep shadows on the path. Fringe cups and red huckleberries add to the forest atmosphere. And wildflowers frolic in the shadows in the spring. If the weather's hot, you may be tempted to linger here.

The pathways in Greenway Park offer smooth walking to stroller-shoving moms.

Leave the trees as you wind onward on the asphalt trail. Oregon white oak and Oregon ash trees sink their roots into the creekbed on the left. Keep an eye on the horizon as you walk. You may spot a great blue heron patrolling the marshy perimeter of Greenway Park. Watching one of these large-bodied birds circling slowly over the wetlands, you might be reminded of the last time you saw a traffic helicopter hovering over a traffic jam.

Stay left at the next junction, then go left again in front of a small basketball court. If you're walking in the summer months, you'll catch the sweet fragrance of the banks of wild roses on the left. Watch for the hubbub of Scholls Ferry Road ahead. Stay left at the next junction, then curve right toward another basketball court. Go right again immediately afterward, and begin your return trip toward Hall Boulevard.

Keep to the main trail straight ahead as secondary trails take off to either side. You'll pass a large group of cattails on the right. Watch for the darting shapes of red-winged blackbirds as you pass. They love to hide among the tall, dense reeds.

Reenter the forest of Oregon ash, then emerge to continue on toward Hall. Skirt a play area (on the left) and a basketball court (on the right), then stay with the main path straight ahead. The way back toward your car is lined with young Douglas firs and deodar cedars. Suburban homes perch along the west edge of the park, spreading their backyards out into the grass.

You'll spot the back wall of Albertson's ahead of you. Push on through open lawns to regain your starting point.

♦ 31 ♦
Hyland Forest Park

Distance: 1 mile (round trip)
Estimated time required: 25 minutes
Highlights: A relaxing loop walk through a pleasant suburban forest
Terrain: Level walking on sawdust-padded path; no wheelchairs, strollers are okay
Best time to go: Spring for wildflowers, fall for leaves, anytime for exercise

Background Hyland Forest Park is a welcome breath of wilderness in the suburban heart of Beaverton. Dive into the shaded recesses of this unexpected forestland, and you'll escape the concrete and asphalt world outside and sense the earth again. Take a walk in Hyland Forest Park on a sunny afternoon or slog through it on a rainy morning. Listen to the songs of birds, the rustling of squirrels, and the whisper of the wind in Douglas firs. Suddenly, you'll feel alive again.

You don't need heavy boots or a stout walking stick for this friendly little forest. Wear your tennis shoes, and bring along your children or a friend. Stroll the 1-mile loop around the park's perimeter, and watch for wildflowers or blackberries or sparrows. Savor the sweetness of the woods as you introduce yourself to Hyland Forest Park. The two of you will be old friends before your walk is finished.

Getting There Hyland Forest Park hides between busy Southwest Murray Boulevard and the equally popular Southwest Hall. The park is skirted on the north by Southwest Hart Road. To reach the start of this walk at Southwest 136th Avenue, just south of Hargis Road, drive south on Highway 217 and take the Allen Boulevard exit. Go west on Allen Boulevard to Murray Boulevard, and turn left. Then turn left onto Hart Road (¾ mile after the Allen/Murray intersection), and drive east to 136th Avenue. Go right on 136th, and continue to the edge of the forest. You can leave your car parked at the trailhead.

No Tri-Met bus lines run along Hyland Forest Park. The closest access is provided by Tri-Met Bus 62. The line follows the course of Southwest Murray Boulevard.

Getting Around The popularity of Hyland Forest Park has combined with the fragile forest understory to make this little wilderness a web of footpaths. Currently, none of the junctions are marked, so it's rather difficult to describe a set walking route. We've attempted to guide you through a walk here, but don't worry if you miss a junction. In Hyland Forest Park, you're never too far away from civilization—but you're far enough!

Leave 136th Avenue, and enter Hyland Forest Park on a sawdust-covered trail. You'll catch the fragrance of the wild roses on the right side of the path

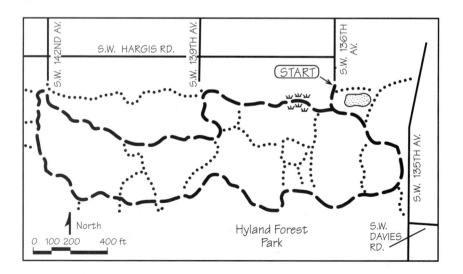

if you're visiting on a spring or summer day. Walk to the junction, and take the second of two trails heading left toward Southwest Davies Road. Fringe cups line the path in May, their cream-colored blossoms hanging like delicate teacups from their long green stems.

Walk beside a marshy pond, and listen for the splashes of fleeing frogs as you continue. Angle right from the water, and climb gently to reach another junction. Keep to the left on the main trail. Oregon grape bushes brighten the forest with their yellow flowers in late March and April. And bigleaf maples whisper overhead, letting their shadows drop like unkept secrets to the ground.

Stay on the main trail as you trace the perimeter of the park. At the junction for Davies Road, veer sharply to the right to continue through the forest. Watch for white blossoms on the thimbleberry bushes as you walk westward. The tangy fruit will be ready for sampling in July. One note of warning—when we hiked here in September, the red berries on the vinelike European bittersweet were abundant. This plant (also known as "nightshade") can be poisonous to humans, so keep a close eye on what your children sample.

Hike on through a forest of thin red alders, and reach another junction, where you'll continue straight. It's fairly easy to discern which is the main, sawdust-padded trail, but smaller pathways fan off to the left and right as you walk. Stay with the main trail on your first visit. If you like this park as much as we do, you'll probably be back to explore again.

Red alders and Douglas firs shelter a forest floor that's sprinkled with trilliums in March and April. Later on, fringe cups, northern inside-out flowers, and Siberian lettuce add their blossoms to the spring extravaganza. Please resist the urge to pluck the flowers, as this park must provide a breath of nature to a host of gasping suburbanites.

Reach a T junction and go left to continue your route around the forest's outer edge. Sword ferns and bracken ferns compete for swaths of sun the greedy vine maples can't consume. Keep to the right at the next junction, and continue beneath a canopy of red alders. You'll pass large banks of Himalayan blackberries on both sides of the trail. Wild strawberries dot the ground with small white blossoms in spring.

Stay along the perimeter path as smaller trails join in from the left and right. The forest floor is carpeted with sword ferns here. Sword ferns are an evergreen plant, so they provide "living color" to the forest all year long. Oregon grape bushes add splashes of bright yellow when they blossom in spring. And the tiny white flowers of Siberian lettuce make the ground a lovely canvas in May and June.

Arrive at a junction where another trail joins in from the right. Stay to the left to walk along the perimeter of the park. You'll hear occasional traffic noise from surrounding streets as you continue on the main trail. Trilliums are abundant along the path in March and April. Descend gently toward the northwest corner of Hyland Forest Park.

A mother and daughter scan the surface of the little pond in Hyland Forest Park.

Salal bushes crowd the trail, boasting pale pink, bell-like flowers in late spring. Salal berries are popular with wildlife; coastal Indians often supplemented their diets with the dark purple fruit.

Curve to the right along the corner of the park, watching for open-bottomed wooden bat houses in the trees. Brown bats are a valuable addition to both forestland and urban areas. A hungry brown bat can consume 500 insects in one hour.

Western starflowers twinkle beside the trail in early June. One look at these six-petaled white blossoms, and you'll realize how the flower got its name. Watch for the large green leaves of the pathfinder plant, too. The triangular greenery is almost white on the underside. Flip a leaf over with an errant footstep, and your path will be marked with a bright arrow.

Walk onward beneath Douglas firs and vine maples, continuing on the main trail through the center of the forest. You'll have the songs of birds to keep you company, and outside traffic noise will be lost among the trees. Reach the exit trail toward 139th Avenue, and continue along the northern border of Hyland Forest Park. Watch for red elderberry bushes beside the path, clinging to their bright red berries in July and August. Indians called the elderberry the "tree of music." They cut and dried the hollow branches to make flutelike whistles.

Sword ferns and bracken ferns line the way as you continue toward your starting point. The path may be a little muddy in this section, but the sawdust carpet helps quite a bit. You'll hear the chatter of lawnmowers and the barking of neighborhood dogs as you hike along the edge of the park, but traffic noise is rarely audible and never too annoying.

Walk on in the shade of several Oregon ash trees. Oregon ash is the only ash species that's a native of the Pacific Northwest. Its leaves are painted in lovely shades of gold and brown in fall. If you're afraid of snakes, you can take refuge beneath these trees. According to an old (and probably undocumented) superstition, poisonous snakes never inhabit the ground beneath an Oregon ash.

Keep to the left as you walk, and reach the junction for 136th Avenue soon afterward. Turn here to regain your starting point. (Note: If you pass the pond a second time, you've gone too far.)

♦ 32 ♦
Tualatin Hills Nature Park

Distance: ½ mile (paved paths); as far as you like on less-developed trails
Estimated time required: 30 minutes (all day, if the forest sucks you in)
Highlights: A delightful stomp through a suburban forest
Terrain: Level, paved trails in the civilized part of the park; rough going in the uncivilized part, with limited stroller and wheelchair access
Best time to go: A dry day in winter or spring (blackberries own the footpaths in summer)

Background Thousands and thousands of people drive by the 180 acres of the Tualatin Hills Nature Park on any given day. Intent on commuting to work or school or supermarket, they hardly even notice this defiant swath of green, fluttering above an area awash in busy roads, high-tech businesses, and stylish suburban dwellings. But life goes on in the forest—noticed or unnoticed. The trilliums still bloom in spring. The deer still leave their footprints in the mud. The real (or imagined?) growls of mountain lions still ride on the breeze. The turtles still swim in Beaverton Creek. And the Oregon white oak trees still soften the pathways with their fallen leaves.

But Tualatin Hills Nature Park will not be overlooked much longer. Way back in 1980, through the combined efforts of local citizens and the Tualatin Hills Parks and Recreation District, the land long known as St. Mary's Woods was obtained from the Catholic archdiocese of Portland. Local, state, and private funding all figured into the purchase.

For almost two decades, lovers and supporters of this forest waited and planned. And, in early 1998, a much more accessible Tualatin Hills Nature Park was unveiled at last. Projects completed included the development of an access route on the east side of the park (along Southwest Millikan Boulevard), the construction of a nature center, and the establishment of a defined trail network.

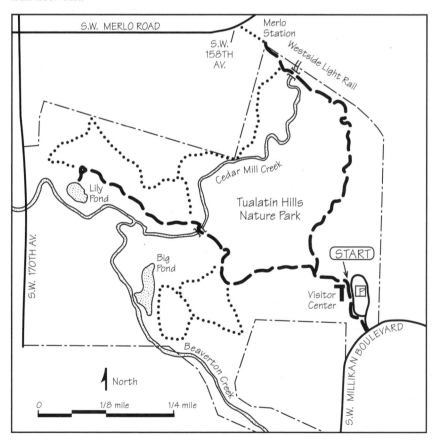

Unfortunately, as this book was being assembled, the initial ½ mile of paved trails was just short of completion, and the planned addition of another 2 miles of gravel-surfaced pathways was still at least a year away. Rather than attempt to provide visitors with a detailed hike we aren't yet able to take ourselves, we've simply included as accurate a map as possible and a loose description of what you'll see when you visit.

Currently, there are some negotiable use trails on the west side of the park (with access off Southwest 170th Avenue). It will be better for the forest if visitors explore the more-developed north and east quadrants first, as it is easy to damage delicate streamside habitats with errant footsteps.

If the short paved path from the information center simply makes you hungry for more, see if you can trace a portion of the trail network planned

Deer tracks are common along the creek in the Tualatin Hills Nature Park.

for completion in 1999. Lace up your oldest pair of tennis shoes. Pull on a long-sleeved shirt to protect your elbows from the blackberries. Wear long pants to guard your ankles from the poison oak. Find a stick to beat away the spider webs. And come experience St. Mary's Woods.

Getting There From downtown Portland, drive west on U.S. Highway 26. Take the Murray Boulevard exit, and drive south to the Tualatin Valley Highway. Go right here, then turn right again on Millikan Boulevard. You'll reach the edge of Tualatin Hills Nature Park soon afterward. Look for a sign, and make a left turn into the paved parking lot beside the information center.

If you're using public transit, Tri-Met Bus 57 runs along the south end of the forest, on the Tualatin Valley Highway. Ask for the Millikan Boulevard stop, and walk north to reach the starting point of the hike. There is also a soon-to-be operable light rail stop, as well as bus connections (Tri-Met Buses 60 and 67), on the north edge of the park (at Merlo Station). The paved trail should extend to here, and you'll be able to reach the nature park's information center with a short walk.

Getting Around Introduce yourself to Tualatin Hills Nature Park with a walk on the paved path that leaves from the information center, then try scouting out some of the gravel-surfaced routes, as well. Here's an idea of what you can expect to see.

The primary tree types in the nature park are Douglas firs, red alders, western red cedars, and Oregon ash. You'll also see many hawthorns and Oregon white oaks. Both Beaverton Creek and Cedar Mill Creek wind through the forest, so the forest floor is usually damp and often muddy. Small ponds offer glimpses of unique animal and plant habitats.

Himalayan blackberries line many of the trails, doing their utmost to claim the sun-sprinkled pathways for themselves. Himalayan blackberries, although delicious, are the scourge of many Northwest wild areas, choking out native plant life in their endless quest for soil and sun.

Watch for friendlier trailing blackberries on the ground, as well. They boast bright white blossoms in the spring. And wild strawberries offer sweet red morsels a little later in the year.

Stinging nettles may make their presence known if you do any bushwhacking here. Between the blackberry bushes, the stinging nettles, and the occasional patches of poison oak, exploring in the undeveloped sections of this forest is discouraged not only by management but also by the underbrush.

Deer are abundant in the forest, at least for now. As visitors to the nature park grow more numerous, you might have to satisfy yourself with an occasional hoof print to verify the deer's continued presence. Watch for raccoon prints, too. Walk quietly, and you might catch a glimpse of a turtle floating with the current in one of the nature park's two creeks.

Wildflowers growing here in early spring include trilliums, false lily of the valley, and cream-colored fringe cups. Yellow buttercups line the way in April and May. In June, the purplish blossoms of Pacific waterleaf wave their long stamens toward the sun, and star flowers, northern inside-out flowers, and vanilla leaf join in.

Oregon grape is a native plant that's abundant in the forest, too. You'll know it by its shiny green leaves and bright yellow blossoms. Sharp-eyed hikers might spot the slender purple petals of tough-leaved irises on occasion. And sword ferns often duel above the delicate white blossoms of Siberian lettuce.

More changes are in store for this wonderful little wilderness in the coming years. With added accessibility, more and more people will come to see the forest's beauty. Please step gently here. The forest is fragile—and worthy of our care.

◆ 33 ◆
Jackson Bottom Wetlands

Distance: 2 miles

Estimated time required: 1 hour

Highlights: Front-line look at a natural area that is gaining ground in its battle with "civilization"

Terrain: Level walking on unpaved, often damp and brushy paths; no strollers or wheelchairs

Best time to go: Early morning for birdwatching; visit after a few days of dry weather if you don't want to get wet

Background According to a recent government estimate, more than 1 million acres of wetlands vanished in the United States during the years between 1985 and 1995. They succumbed to housing developments, shopping malls, landfills, and pavement. Why is this a big deal? Wetlands are a crucial habitat for a host of fish, birds, and other wildlife. Wetlands are an essential link in the chain of natural purification that keeps streams and rivers from being overcome by pollutants. And wetlands serve an important role in preventing or minimizing the devastation of flooding during times of heavy rain or snow runoff. Is Jackson Bottom Wetlands worth protecting? You bet it is!

Fortunately, a handful of groups and agencies are working together to preserve this small wetlands area just south of downtown Hillsboro, along the shore of the Tualatin River. The Unified Sewerage Agency (an organization dedicated to the cleanup of the Tualatin River), the City of Hillsboro,

A covered viewing platform provides a dry refuge for birdwatchers and hikers.

Metro, area schools, and a concerned citizens group all work together to protect and provide access to Jackson Bottom Wetlands.

A hike here won't wear you out. The area is too small, and the trail options are too limited. But it will open your eyes. You'll see the beauty of birds in flight; you'll see the loveliness and the fragility of the wetlands habitat; and you'll see what a little positive action can do to preserve a natural treasure we can't live without.

Getting There To reach Jackson Bottom Wetlands, follow the Tualatin Valley Highway through downtown Hillsboro. Turn left on South First Avenue (Southwest Hillsboro Highway, Highway 219), and drive about 1¼ miles to a sign for Jackson Bottom Wetlands. There's a small unpaved parking lot on the left side of the road, just before a bridge across the Tualatin River. Portable toilets, a viewing platform, and an informational signboard are the only amenities provided, at present.

Currently, there is no public bus service to Jackson Bottom Wetlands.

Getting Around Before you descend into Jackson Bottom, you may want to pause at the viewing platform on the east side of the parking lot to look out over the wetlands and get your bearings. In the foreground is Kingfisher Marsh, the main body of water here. Beyond the marsh, the Jackson Slough slogs its way toward a rendezvous with the Tualatin River (on the right). And beyond that is a retention pond, utilized for water treatment and wildlife habitat.

If you're fortunate enough to visit on a clear day, you should have a magnificent view of Mount Hood soaring skyward in the distance. There is much to be said for visiting here on a clear (and rainless) day, as many of the trails burrow through waist-high grasses, sure to soak you if they're wet. Come early in the day if you want the best opportunities for bird and wildlife viewing. No dogs or bicycles are allowed in the wetlands, and it's a good idea to bring along a friend for company and security.

Leave the south corner of the parking lot on the signed Kingfisher Marsh Trail, and descend a set of wooden steps. Then continue straight on a path lined with Oregon ash and Himalayan blackberries. In late summer, the blackberries will assail you with their fragrance (and their thorns). Look for the white globes of snowberries (not edible) and the blue blossoms of chicory, as well. Chicory is a relative of Belgian endive—salad, anyone?

You'll notice many waist-high wooden posts beside the trails here. Although some are empty, many are decorated with the handiwork of local students. Pause to ponder the poems or study the brief reports on food chains, habitat, and bird life, and you'll appreciate the fact that this wetlands is also a valuable educational tool and very probably a great field-trip destination.

Birdhouses cling to scores of tree trunks in the Jackson Bottom Wetlands.

Parallel the shore of the often-murky Tualatin River as you walk on. Once woefully polluted, this 83-mile long waterway that flows into the Willamette River near Oregon City has enjoyed a renaissance in the past decade. One glance at the dark water and you'll be pretty sure there's still much room for improvement. But talk to one of the trout fishers stalking the banks, and he or she will tell you—this river is coming alive again.

The riverside trail is hung with the white blossoms of oceanspray in spring. If you have children along, be sure to steer them away from the red berries on the European bittersweet (also known as "nightshade"), prevalent in the summer months.

Birdhouses and bat houses hang on scores of trees as you walk on. Enter more open terrain, and angle right at the Y to stay beside the river for a time. Listen for the songs of birds, the humming of the crickets, and the whisper of wind in the marsh grass, and be sure to keep an eye on the sky for great blue herons, hawks, and swallows passing overhead.

Come to a three-way junction (please be forewarned—these trails can change at the whim of the lawnmower driver), and continue straight to stay with a meandering route toward the Kingfisher Marsh viewing platform. If you're in a hurry or more interested in birdwatching than in wetlands wandering, take the path to the left for a more direct route to the platform.

Walk past blossom-laden hawthorns and wild roses, following the riverbank trail. Keep right at the next junction to visit "Vic's Grove," a corner of Jackson Bottom Wetlands dedicated to Vic Madsen. According to the dedication plaque, he planted trees here on the last day of his 90-year-long

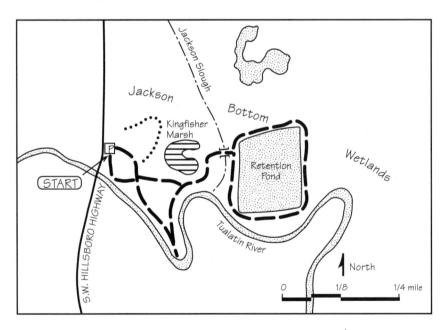

life. Angle left beneath Oregon ash and bigleaf maples to arrive at a view-point above the river, then backtrack to the junction and go right to head out toward the viewing platform above the marsh.

The path is brushy and sometimes nearly obscured by grass. Arrive at the Kingfisher Marsh viewing platform and enjoy a 360-degree view around the wetlands. We spotted a beaver and several geese in the waters here. You might see a swan, a heron, or a parade of ducks. If you didn't bring your binoculars, kick yourself down the stairs and hike on.

Continue with the grass-edged trail to cross Jackson Slough on a sturdy footbridge. It's possible to make a loop around the retention pond from here. Go in either direction to make your circle. We headed out in a counterclock-wise direction, passing a nice viewpoint where the slough flows into the Tualatin River, then pushing on past a birdhouse bonanza in the trees. Wherever you wander, please stay on established paths. Be especially quiet during nesting season, when the birdhouses are also nurseries.

Return to the bridge to recross the slough, then backtrack to your starting point.

♦ 34 ♦
Lower Macleay Park

Distance: 2 miles (round trip)
Estimated time required: 1 hour
Highlights: Wonderful forest setting with the captivating company of Balch Creek
Terrain: Gentle inclines on mostly unpaved trails; a short section is accessible to wheelchairs and strollers, but the remainder of the hike is rough going
Best time to go: The wildflowers are enchanting in April and May; fall brings its own finery

Background If you're looking for a city walk with a wilderness feel to it, visit Lower Macleay Park sometime soon—and take a local "walk on the wild side." The trail through Lower Macleay Park will lead you into the forested depths of Balch Canyon, and you'll hike beneath massive Douglas firs and towering cedars as you climb beside chortling Balch Creek. This cascade-studded waterway is the largest stream in Forest Park. Its banks support a plethora of wildflowers, and the hillsides on either side of it are thick with trees.

Lower Macleay Park offers a refuge from the hustle and bustle of the city.

In 1897, Donald Macleay, a Portland banker and civic leader, donated 107 acres of land to the city of Portland, with the understanding that this land was to become a city park. The acreage of Balch Canyon and its immediate surroundings thus became Macleay Park. Macleay Park was assimilated into larger Forest Park in 1947.

The 25+ mile Wildwood Trail traverses Macleay Park on its journey south from the vicinity of the St. Johns Bridge to Pittock Mansion, Washington Park, and the World Forestry Center. It's possible to link this hike with Walks 5 and 6 by utilizing the connecting trail that descends to Northwest Cornell Road from Pittock Mansion. We've written this walk as a self-contained loop. Try it once this way, then feel free to make adjustments.

You'll be hiking on a dirt trail for most of the trip, so wear boots or washable tennis shoes if the weather's wet. Pushing a stroller on this route would be a challenge, but it's definitely possible. There are restroom facilities at the parking lot, but they're usually locked.

Getting There Reach the trailhead into Lower Macleay Park at the intersection of Northwest Upshur Street and Northwest 29th Avenue. There's a small parking lot just west of the intersection. This is a popular launching point for Forest Park joggers, as well as hikers and picnickers. If you come on a sunny weekend, you may have to scramble for a parking spot.

Tri-Met Bus 17 runs along Northwest Vaughn Street, one block north of Upshur. You can get off at Montgomery Park, then walk south on Northwest 27th Avenue to reach Upshur. Follow Upshur west to the park entrance. Tri-Met Bus 15 is another good option. Ask for the stop closest to the Thurman Street Bridge, and descend to the park via the stairway at the east end of the span.

Getting Around Before you get started on your walk, pause to read the historical marker on the boulder at the entrance to the parking lot. It'll provide you with some background information on Balch Canyon. Proceed to the south end of the parking area, and begin your hike on an asphalt path; you'll see the historic Thurman Street Bridge above you. The original bridge was built in the 1890s as a simple wooden span across Balch Canyon. That structure was replaced with the current steel bridge in 1903 as part of the flurry of construction heralding the Lewis and Clark Exposition of 1905.

Walk beneath the Thurman Street Bridge, and stay on the asphalt as you head into the woods. Donald Macleay assumed that the land he'd given to the city of Portland would be logged, and he stipulated that funds from timber sales were to go to Portland hospitals. Fortunately for Portland's wilderness-loving walkers, much of the land was left undisturbed, and the city policy has leaned toward preservation rather than exploitation of the lovely forest that fills Balch Canyon.

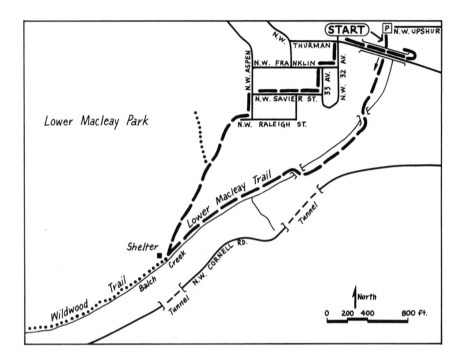

The hillsides on either side of the canyon are green with bigleaf maples and cottonwoods. Walk beside the rushing waters of Balch Creek on your left. If you're hiking in the spring, watch for the flower-studded spires of fringe cups on the embankment to the right. Sword ferns prick the air with their green tips, as well.

Gain a dirt footpath when the asphalt disappears. The traffic noise from Thurman Street soon sinks beneath the chortle of the water, and the songs of birds are interwoven with the whisper of the flowing stream. The air beside the creek is cool and sweet, freshly scrubbed by the passage of the water.

Veer to the left to cross Balch Creek on a sturdy wooden footbridge. Watch for the thin green stalks of common horsetail in the damp earth beside the water. (Its informal name is potscrubber plant.) In May, the delicate white blooms of Siberian lettuce add their color to the shoreline. You'll know Siberian lettuce by its five-petaled flowers, streaked with tiny lines of pink.

False Solomon's seal is another common wildflower when spring arrives. The blossoms grow on long green stems, standing above the mossy forest floor. Press your nose against a flower and inhale. You'll swear someone doused the blossom with perfume. Smith's fairybell is yet another wildflower you'll find here in April, May, and June. Watch for the white, bell-shaped flowers ringing out their melodies across the hillsides.

Climb steadily and gain a little height above the stream. The fissures of the bigleaf maple trunks are carpeted with soft green moss, and ferns sprout from the crevices, giving witness to the dampness of the canyon. Watch for the three-petaled faces of trilliums along the hillside in March and April.

Pass a lovely little waterfall as the trail becomes more level, then note a long-dead western red cedar just beyond it to the right of the trail. The cedar's branchless trunk pierces the open sky above it, ending in a sharpened point. Loggers call these dead trees "widow makers" because they're dangerous when left standing. Despite all that, this tree is lovely, thanks to the glowing green moss that lives on its dead shell.

Continue on (quickly, if it's windy!) and climb beside the water. Western hemlocks and English holly bushes line the trail. Scores of toppled trees clutter the forest floor, making a sober backdrop for the cheerful fairybells. Keep an eye out for the bright pink blossoms of salmonberry bushes if you're walking in late April.

Reach a double set of footbridges, and cross the creek again. Watch for a large western hemlock on the right side of the trail, not long afterward. Yellow stream violets and false Solomon's seal line the path as you continue. Climb steadily beneath massive Douglas firs. Look for two sturdy fellows on the hillside to the right, just before you walk beside one of their fallen cohorts.

A little later on, you'll see another huge Douglas fir on the left side of the trail. This giant measures 18 feet around its trunk, chest-high off the ground. Continue on the creekside trail to reach a dilapidated stone building, ruling a three-way junction. This run-down shelter was built by the Civilian Conservation Corps in the 1930s. Its walls show the scars of repeated breaches by ferns and graffiti artists.

Veer sharply to the right at the junction. You'll join the Wildwood Trail as you climb the canyon hillside and leave the cool environs of Balch Creek behind. (By the way, if you're looking for different ways to enjoy the hiking opportunities in Macleay Park on future excursions, try the trail straight ahead someday. It leads across Northwest Cornell Road and onward and upward to Pittock Mansion.)

Ascend steadily along the hillside. Vanilla leaf, false Solomon's seal, and fringe cups decorate the ground with springtime blossoms. Red elderberry bushes are abundant in this area, as well. Watch for their bright berries in the summer.

A special treat awaits you if you take this hike in May or June. Look for the showy purple blossoms of tough-leaved irises hiding in the grass. These beautiful flowers look like escapees from the local florist shop. They seem much too sophisticated to be growing wild on the hillside.

Come a little later in the year, and you'll have another treat in store. Tangled trails of wild strawberries crisscross the slope, offering their bite-sized bits of fruit to hungry hikers. You'll gain more open terrain as you continue up. Red huckleberry bushes crowd the trail, competing with sword ferns for the sun that filters through the Douglas firs.

Stay on the main trail as you skirt the edge of an open meadow. If you're looking for a sunny picnic spot, this peaceful square of grass is it. Reach a junction marked for Holman Lane. Leave Wildwood Trail and turn right onto Holman Lane, descending slightly to reach a metal gate. Take the path around the gate, and continue along the far edge of the meadow to reach a second barrier.

You'll emerge on Northwest Raleigh Street. Walk to the intersection and turn left on Northwest Aspen Avenue, passing attractive homes along the way. Hike along Aspen to Northwest Savier Street, where you'll turn right. Continue on Savier and plunge steeply downhill after the first block. If the day is clear, you'll have an impressive view of east Portland and Mount Hood from here. Turn left off Savier onto Northwest 33rd Avenue, walk a block, then turn right onto Northwest Franklin Court. Go left again onto Northwest 32nd Avenue, continuing down the hill.

Cross busy Northwest Thurman Street, and turn right to hike along its northern edge. Walk above Lower Macleay Park on the historic Thurman Street Bridge. Pause to read the small plaque in the center of the span, and be sure to scan the horizon for glimpses of Mount St. Helens, Mount Rainier, and Mount Adams. All three are visible on a clear day.

At the far end of the bridge, turn left to descend a hidden set of stairs that will bring you back to the park and your starting point.

◆ 35 ◆
Sauvie Island—Oak Island

Distance: 2⅔ miles (round trip)
Estimated time required: 1 hour and 20 minutes
Highlights: Wild roses and beautiful old oaks; a pleasant pasture walk
Terrain: Level, grassy path; no wheelchairs or strollers
Best time to go: This hike is closed for hunting from mid-October to mid-
   January; the rest of the year, go anytime you want a quiet stroll

Background Sauvie Island is a large, extremely fertile piece of land, bounded on the east by the Columbia River and on the west by Multnomah Channel. Situated near the point where the Willamette River flows into the broad Columbia (see Walk 9, Kelley Point Park), Sauvie Island has been blessed by nature with a double dose of rich, dark river silt. As a result, this island boasts the most fertile farmland in Oregon. And acres of pumpkins, vegetables, grain crops, and berry bushes cover its southern half.

In the northern reaches of the island, lakes, marshes, and open fields provide a comfortable domain for birds and animals. The Oregon Department of Fish and Wildlife currently administers 12,000 acres of Sauvie Island, and

An Oregon white oak on Oak Island

the land is a home or resting place for more than 250 species of birds.

In the fall, 300,000 ducks and geese stop off on Sauvie Island. Thousands of sandhill cranes pass through each year, and Portland's city bird, the great blue heron, is a regular visitor to the island's Sturgeon Lake. Earthbound residents of Sauvie Island include black-tailed deer, raccoons, red foxes, rabbits, and squirrels. There are 12 documented species of harmless amphibians and reptiles on the island, too.

But Sauvie Island has a history that goes back well beyond pumpkin patches or the Fish and Wildlife Department. For centuries, the island was the seasonal home of the Multnomah Indians. The Indians hunted and fished in the island's forests and lakes, and they gathered the island's wappato plant for food. At one time, the wappato plant was abundant on Sauvie Island. Indians collected this "wild potato" in the island's marshes and along the edges of the ponds, then they roasted the starchy roots to supplement their diet of fruit and meat.

As a matter of fact, the wappato plant gave Sauvie Island one of its first names known to the white man. The exploring duo of Lewis and Clark paused here on their journey to the Pacific Ocean, and they named the place Wappato Island after being served roasted tubers by the Multnomah Indians.

The name that has stayed with the island through the twentieth century is Sauvie Island, though. That title comes from a French Canadian settler named Laurent Sauvé. Sauvé operated a dairy for the Hudson Bay Company on the island in the mid 1800s. The dairy supplied cheese and milk to Fort Vancouver, just up the Columbia River. Eventually, the Hudson Bay Company pulled out, and the first generation of Sauvie farmers moved in.

But farming on the island was a risky and sometimes unrewarding business because of yearly flooding by the Columbia. The U.S. Army Corps of Engineers completed a system of dikes on Sauvie Island in 1941. Those dikes resulted in the cessation of Sauvie's annual floods. Unfortunately, they also contributed to the demise of the water-loving wappato.

This hike on Oak Island provides a good look into Sauvie Island's watery history. You'll walk on a grassy peninsula ruled by a stand of ancient oaks, and you'll be surrounded by ponds and lakes on every side. Keep an eye out for waterfowl as you walk. Wood ducks, Canada geese, and great blue herons are frequent visitors to the shores of Sturgeon Lake.

If you come early in the day, you may want to wear boots or waterproof footwear, as the grass can be long and dewy. Otherwise, tennis shoes should be adequate. Please note that this area is closed to hikers from mid-October

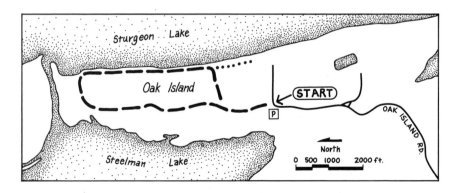

to mid-January, and a parking permit is required. You can purchase a one-day or a seasonal permit at various outlets (one source is the little island store near the Sauvie Island Bridge), or call the Oregon Department of Fish and Wildlife for more information.

Getting There Unfortunately, Tri-Met buses don't serve this part of Sauvie Island. To reach the walk by car, take the Sauvie Island Bridge off U.S. Highway 30. Go north on Northwest Sauvie Island Road, then turn right on Northwest Reeder Road. Follow Reeder Road to Oak Island Road and turn left. Drive north on quiet Oak Island Road, lose the pavement, and continue straight at the four-way junction near the pond. Rattle onward to the road's termination, 5 miles from the intersection with Reeder Road.

Getting Around Leave the parking area by continuing straight on the entry road (north). You'll see what look like three possible routes fanning out in front of you—take the middle trail. (On our most recent visit, it was marked with small signs denoting a hiker.) The route is somewhat overgrown, and wild roses grow in fragrant tangles on either side. You'll marvel at the massive Oregon white oaks you pass as you begin. There's a particularly interesting oak trunk on the left side of the path. The deeply furrowed wood is twisted into an agonizing knot of angles and curves.

Continue walking north on the overgrown road. If you're visiting in spring or summer, you'll be surrounded by the pink blossoms of wild roses. Listen for the voices of the birds as you work your way out along the peninsula. You'll hear the squawks of pheasants, the calls of mallards, and the honks of geese.

Pass a large stand of Oregon white oaks on the left side of the trail. The wooden houses nailed onto the trunks are the homes of island wood ducks. As you continue on the grass-covered road, you'll begin to see water on the left. This is part of Steelman Lake. The green hills in the distance hold the city of Scappoose.

Enter an open meadow (if you're a hay-fever sufferer, you may want to avoid this walk in spring and summer), and follow the grassy track straight ahead. You'll pass a lone oak tree on the left side of the road. If the day's a sunny one, look for a swarm of activity around a knothole about ¾ of the way up the trunk. Wild honey, anyone?

Angle left as you continue beside a forest of Oregon white oaks. Pass a thicket of Himalayan blackberries, then wind through a stand of tall black cottonwoods. You'll see Oregon ash trees sprinkled in among the cottonwoods and oaks. These trees have massive, rough-barked trunks, and their leaves are beautiful in autumn.

Stay on the swath cut through the grass as you curve around the oak forest. You'll emerge on the shore of Sturgeon Lake and continue to the right. Watch for great blue herons as you walk. The herons are very shy, so you'll have to admire their gently flapping forms as they flee from your advance. No matter how many times you've seen a great blue heron in the air, you'll ask the same question as you watch it lumber into takeoff—how does that creature ever get its gangly body off the ground?

Continue around the perimeter of the oak forest. The twisted trunks rear hauntingly sculptured silhouettes against the sky. If the day is clear, you'll have a feast for your eyes on the horizon. Both Mount Adams and Mount St. Helens are visible on this hike. Arrive at the south end of the thick oak forest, and turn right onto a wide swath cut into the grass. It's just opposite a rocky beach and should be marked by another hiking symbol. (If you reach the "No Entry" sign, you've gone too far.) Walk west to close the loop toward your car.

If your legs need a break, you can pause at the small wooden bench and memorial on the right side of the path. It honors a young man who loved Sauvie Island. Sit awhile and perhaps you'll fall in love as well. Then walk on beside more oaks, keeping an eye out for wild rabbits as you go. Cross a pathway angling in from the left, and continue straight on your overgrown trail.

Regain your entry route as you emerge onto the road along the west side of the woods. Go left to retrace your footsteps to your car.

◆ 36 ◆
Sauvie Island–Virginia Lake

Distance: 2¼ miles (round trip)
Estimated time required: 1 hour and 15 minutes
Highlights: Glimpses of great blue herons, geese, and ducks
Terrain: Level walking on dirt and grass; no strollers or wheelchairs
Best time to go: Pleasant any time of year

Background   Refer to Walk 35 for general information on Sauvie Island. This walk around Virginia Lake is special for one reason—birds. If you want to get a close-up look at a great blue heron, Virginia Lake is a super place to hike. Step softly and always keep one eye on the skyline as you walk. Other birds are abundant here, as well. You'll probably spot several Canada geese if you're walking in the fall. Wood ducks nest among the Oregon ash trees in the surrounding forest, and you'll see a variety of smaller birds if you're observant.

If you own a pair of binoculars, be sure to bring them on this walk, and carry water if the day is warm. There are several nice picnic spots along the perimeter of Virginia Lake, so plan to stop for lunch if you can spare the time. One more thing—much of the Virginia Lake area is marshland, so wear old shoes or boots and leave an extra pair of socks back at the car.

Getting There Unfortunately, Tri-Met buses don't serve this part of Sauvie Island. To reach the walk by car, take the Sauvie Island Bridge off U.S. Highway 30. Go north on Northwest Sauvie Island Road, pass the intersection with Northwest Reeder Road, and continue. Watch for Sauvie Island Wildlife Refuge Headquarters on the right side of the road (there's a sign). The turnoff for the Wapato Access Greenway is ⅓ mile farther.

Not far past the intersection with Ferry Road, watch for a small gravel parking pulloff on the left side of the road, just as the pavement angles to the right. (It's signed for the "Wapato Access Greenway.") You can leave your car in the lot while you hike, but you will need a parking permit. You can purchase a one-day or a seasonal permit at various outlets (one source is the little island store near the Sauvie Island Bridge), or call the Oregon Department of Fish and Wildlife for more information.

Getting Around Leave the parking area on an overgrown road (behind the metal gate) that heads toward Multnomah Channel. Angle to the right along a stand of trees. You'll arrive at a wooden picnic shelter on the shore of marshy Virginia Lake. Pass along the left (south) side of the shelter as you walk toward the river. You'll gain an overgrown road descending gently beside a bank of Himalayan blackberries.

Angle left with the road, and pass a footpath shooting off to the right as you hike along the lake's swampy perimeter. Continue along the overgrown road, paralleling the shore of the lake. Walk beneath the spreading branches of a massive Oregon white oak, and descend gently to curve around the south end of the lake. You'll join a more defined roadway as you walk toward the river. Continue on in the shade of Oregon ash trees, black cottonwoods, and

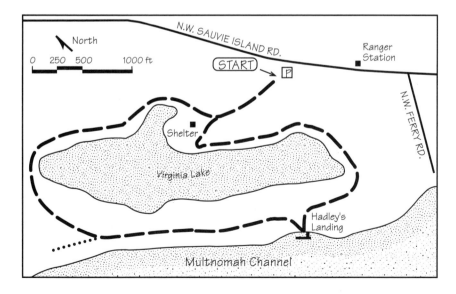

Two walkers pause over a map of Sauvie Island on a sunlit shoreline.

scattered hawthorns. Note the bird blind/viewing platform on the right.

Just before you leave the edge of Virginia Lake and enter the riverside forest, scan the water one more time. We surprised two herons wading in the shallows here—or perhaps it was the herons that surprised us. There's nothing quite like the sight of one of these big creatures as it fights its way into the air, flapping its long wings in unlikely flight. Walk silently and watch!

Hike on toward the river and arrive at a Y in the trail. Continue to the right, paralleling the riverbank. (If you have the energy, make the short jaunt to the left to visit Hadley's Landing, a public boat landing that's part of the Willamette Greenway access system. There's a plaque in the small clearing beside the dock that provides some background information on the spot.) Continue your walk around Virginia Lake by wandering north along the riverside path.

You'll be walking in the shade of tall black cottonwoods, and Himalayan blackberries and wild roses lie in tangles on the forest floor. Watch for the bright crimson berries of red elderberry bushes in the summer months. White snowberries glow in the forest gloom in August, and the delicate yellow blossoms of touch-me-not decorate the shadows into fall.

You may hear the muted rumble of the trucks on U.S. Highway 30, just across the water, and you'll surely have the roar of powerboats to keep you company if you're walking on a sunny weekend day. For the most part, though, you'll be alone with the whisper of the cottonwoods and the songs of forest birds as you continue along the shore of Multnomah Channel.

Stay straight on the main path as a secondary trail shoots off to the right, then curve along the edge of an open meadow where aged Oregon ash trees sink their roots into the knee-high grass. Pass a large stand of Pacific willows, and continue to a fork in the trail. Take the branch to the right, and angle inland between banks of wild roses and Himalayan blackberries.

Go right again to walk across a wooden footbridge raised above the swampy ground. The sound of your footsteps will bring on a chorus of peeps and plunks, as the tiny frogs in the shallows dive for cover. Keep an eye out for marsh birds as you continue, and look for wappato blossoms along the north edge of the lake. Climb a gentle incline on a dirt path, then angle right along the west side of Virginia Lake.

Stay beside a bank of Himalayan blackberries as you walk south through a large pasture sprinkled with old Douglas firs. The presence of the trees is a good indication that this piece of ground has probably always been above the fluctuating water level. Most likely, it's one of the spots where the Multnomah Indians camped when they came to the island to hunt and gather the potatolike wappato plant.

Follow an overgrown track through the field as you stay beside the blackberry thicket. Watch for a massive Oregon white oak on the right as you continue. Swing gently away from the blackberries to pass between two oak trees on the overgrown path. Walk beside a needle-topped Douglas fir snag. If you're hiking in June, watch for sprinklings of blue-pod lupine in the grass.

Descend slightly beside a stand of Pacific willows, and stay with the overgrown track as you continue. Approach the shoreline of Virginia Lake, and curve right with the road to turn west. Smaller footpaths shoot off to the sides as you approach the picnic shelter. Angle left with the road before you reach the structure, and head back toward the parking area and your car.

◆ **37** ◆
Sauvie Island—Warrior Rock

Distance: 6 miles (round trip)
Estimated time required: 2½ hours
Highlights: Beach treasures and river scenes
Terrain: Level dirt and sand; no wheelchairs or strollers
Best time to go: A cool spot on a hot summer day, but wonderfully lonely on winter mornings

Background Refer to Walk 35 for general information on Sauvie Island. The hike to Warrior Rock Lighthouse follows the east shore of Sauvie Island, traversing game management land on the way to Warrior Rock, a small lava flow on the island's northern tip.

A representative of the Hudson Bay Company, Lieutenant Broughton, gave the rock its name in the early 1800s. The "Warrior" designation can probably be attributed to Broughton's role as a mediator between the island's Indian population and the white settlers who raised dairy cattle on the land. (By the way, this is the same Broughton who named Oregon's beloved Mount Hood and who lent his name to Broughton Beach on the Columbia River.)

Hot sunshine makes this walk a delightful beachside jaunt on summer afternoons. Wear old tennis shoes, and bring along a Frisbee and a towel. You'll undoubtedly have wet sand between your toes before you're finished. If you're taking children along, you might want to leave some dry clothes in the car.

Foggy fall mornings are a treat on Sauvie Island, too. You'll appreciate the solitude that "off-season" walking will provide as you hike beside the Columbia River on the island's eastern flank. Dress warmly, as the damp air can be chilly. If you're lucky, the sun will burn through the fog by the time you reach Warrior Rock. Be sure to pack a picnic lunch for your stop at the small lighthouse.

There's no drinking water available on the walk, so carry your own liquids. The only restroom facility (a porta-potty) is at the parking lot that marks the hike's start. Please note that a parking permit is required here, as with the other hikes on Sauvie Island. (See the introductions to Walks 35 and 36 for details).

Getting There Unfortunately, Tri-Met buses don't serve this part of Sauvie Island. To reach the walk by car, take the Sauvie Island Bridge off U.S. Highway 30. Go north on Northwest Sauvie Island Road, then turn right on Northwest Reeder Road. Follow Reeder Road to the east side of the island, then continue north along the shore. Reeder Road is unpaved beyond Walton Beach. Drive along the graveled route until it ends at a parking lot. This is the spot!

Getting Around Leave the parking lot from the northeast corner, keeping a sharp eye out for cow pies as you walk beside a meadow sprinkled with grazing bovines. Although the Hudson Bay Company's dairy operation has been gone for more than 140 years, Sauvie Island is still cattle-company country. So watch your step!

Depending on your preference (and the water level), you can walk on the bank above the beach or slog through the sand beside the water as you continue north from the parking lot. To get a feel for both habitats, try the riverside route on your way to the lighthouse, then take the upper path on your return. Stay close to the river to find the firmest sand. If the going gets

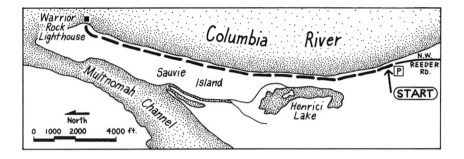

too soggy, you can scramble up the bank to gain the inland route.

If the day is clear, you'll see the white form of Warrior Rock Lighthouse at the far end of a 3-mile stretch of sand. To the north and east, Mount St. Helens and Mount Adams are also visible. Snow-frocked Mount St. Helens paints a lovely picture above the wide Columbia.

Watch for the tall black cottonwood trees lining the beach as you set out. The black cottonwood is the largest deciduous tree in the Pacific Northwest. If you have a sensitive nose, you should be able to catch a whiff of the tree's pleasant balsam fragrance (strongest in the spring) as you pass. The exposed root systems of the cottonwoods are a photographer's dream. Twisted strands of wood burrow into the sand, looking like a dark-haired child's tangled braids.

After about ⅓ mile of walking, keep an eye out for Himalayan blackberry bushes on the riverbank to the left. The berries are succulent in August, fat and dark and moist. But the blackberry bushes are even better in October. Then they're a feast for the eyes. The dying leaves are especially beautiful— dressed in gold and crimson. And leftover berries hide among the finery, offering sweet fall treats to hungry hikers.

Because it's bounded by the Columbia River on one side and Multnomah Channel on the other, Sauvie Island is often draped by thick morning fogs, even when the rest of Portland basks in sunshine. If you're strictly a fair-weather walker, you may want to wait until the afternoon to visit. But you'll be missing some of the greatest pleasures of the walk if you do. When the beach is draped with fog, there's a universe at your feet.

Watch for animal tracks as you walk across the sand. The woods of Sauvie Island shelter raccoons and foxes and black-tailed deer. You may not see them here, but you'll find their footprints in the sand. The island's birds will tantalize you with their prints, as well. Great blue heron tracks are a common sight. (The island's Sturgeon Lake is a popular feeding ground for Portland's official bird.) More than 250 species of birds live on or visit Sauvie Island. Watch for the prints of sandhill cranes, ducks, geese, and gulls.

If you have children hiking with you, they'll quickly teach you how to enjoy a foggy beach. Feathers and shells and bits of cork, mysterious planks

A hiker walks in the footsteps of a great blue heron on the way to Warrior Rock.

and rusted cables—each item is a castaway treasure to a child's eyes. After your children's pockets are filled, they'll start in on yours. If you'd like to do your part for beach ecology (and let your kids earn their after-hike ice cream money at the same time) bring along a plastic garbage sack. Thirty empty cans will buy the family a round of popsicles—and a better Warrior Rock walk.

You'll hear many different river voices as you continue north along the sand—the calls of geese, the bickering of gulls, the rumble of ships' engines in the channel. Traffic noise drifts across the water from the Washington shore, and the long warning blasts of freight trains pierce the quiet as you walk. After about 3 miles, you'll see little Warrior Rock Lighthouse just ahead. Pass an old abandoned homestead just before you get to Warrior Rock. The house was inhabited by Coast Guard personnel when the lighthouse was a staffed facility. The structure and the land around it are private property, so resist the temptation to explore and head for the lighthouse instead.

Warrior Rock is a great spot for a picnic. You'll probably share the little headland with a couple of other hikers and a fisherman or two. And you may have to offer your bread crusts to an inquisitive gull. But chances are you won't mind the company a bit. And the view out across the river will entertain you with passing ships and tugs, the flight of island birds, and the magic of the sunlight on the water.

To regain the parking lot, take the small dirt road back along the riverbank. You'll pass through a wooded area of Oregon ash, black cottonwoods, and Pacific willows. In spring and summer, the forest floor is green with Himalayan blackberries, red huckleberry bushes, and plenty of red and blue elderberry. In June, the perky blossoms of foxglove line the road. This showy flower is the source of the heart medicine digitalis.

Even with all the greenery, you'll have several glimpses of the river as you walk. And the songs of island birds will accompany you as you continue. Emerge from the forest, and hike across an open meadow to reach the parking lot.

Index

B

Broughton, Lieutenant 182
Burntbridge Creek Greenway 59–62

C

Council Crest 31, 34–35
Crystal Springs Rhododendron
    Garden 113, 118

D

Duniway, Abigail Scott 20
Duniway Park 20
Durham, Albert Alonzo 136

E

Elk Point Viewpoint 22
Elk Rock 126
Elk Rock Island 122–127

F

Fanno, Augustus 152
Fanno Farm House 152–155
Forest Park 12, 36, 171

G

Gabriel Park 144–148
George Rogers Park 136–139
Glendoveer Fitness Course 82–87
Greenway Park 152–156
Grotto, The 72–75

H

Himes, George 22, 24
Himes Park 23–26
Hoyt Arboretum 36, 38–39, 44–45
Hyland Forest Park 156–160

I

International Rose Test Garden 36

J

Jackson Bottom Wetlands 164–169
Japanese Garden 36–38, 46
Johnson, Tideman 119

K

Kelley, Hall J. 55
Kelley Point Park 55–58
Kerr, Peter 126

L

Lacamas Park 66–71
Laurelhurst Park 19, 88–92
Lewis and Clark 49, 58, 176
Loop, 40-Mile 12, 23, 31, 38, 52,
    98, 121
Lower Macleay Park 170–174

M

Macleay, Donald 171
Marquam Nature Park 31–35
Marquam Nature Trail 31–35
Marshall Park 128–131
Mill Ends Park 12
Mount Tabor Park 92–98
Multnomah Indians 176, 181

O

Oak Island 174–178
Oaks Bottom Wildlife Refuge 107–
    113
Olmsted, John 19, 88
Oxbow Regional Park 103–107

P

Pittock Mansion 40–41
Powell Butte Nature Park 98–103

R

Reed College 113–119
Reed, Simeon 113
Rose City Golf Course 77–82
Ross Island 30, 110

S

Salmon Creek Greenway 63–66
Sauve, Laurent 176
Sauvie Island 174–185
Smith and Bybee Lakes Natural Area 51–55
Springwater Corridor 119–121
Sturgeon Lake 175–177, 183

T

Terwilliger Boulevard 19–22

Tideman-Johnson Park 119–122
Tryon Creek State Park 131–136
Tualatin Hills Nature Park 160–164

U

University of Portland 47–51

V

Virginia Lake 178–181

W

Warrior Rock 181–185
Warrior Rock Lighthouse 182–185
Washington Park 36
Wildwood Trail 37–40, 45–46, 171, 173–174
Willamette Greenway Trail 28–31
Willamette Park 27–28
Woods Memorial Park 148–152
World Forestry Center 42–43,

About the Authors

Terry and Karen Whitehill begain writing outdoor guidebooks in 1984, starting off more than a decade of adventures with a year-long cycling trip in Europe. They followed this journey with hiking adventures in California, Oregon, Europe, and the Middle East. A return to Europe with their 2-year-old daughter, Sierra, was yet another challenge. The Whitehills then settled down to write about their hometown of Portland, Oregon.

Nature Walks In and Around Portland is the latest of five titles the Whitehills have written for The Mountaineers. The others are *Europe by Bike, France by Bike, Best Short Hikes in California's Northern Sierra,* and *Best Short Hikes in California's Southern Sierra.*

Photo by Mike Luthy.

Karen has a B.A. in English Literature from Portland State University and an M.A. in journalism from the University of Oregon. Terry has a degree in Construction Engineering Managment from Oregon State University.

The Whitehills live in Portland with their three children, Sierra (age 9), Rocky (age 5), and Aliya (age 2).

THE MOUNTAINEERS, founded in 1906, is a nonprofit outdoor activity and conservation club, whose mission is "to explore, study, preserve, and enjoy the natural beauty of the outdoors. . . . " Based in Seattle, Washington, the club is now the third-largest such organization in the United States, with 15,000 members and five branches throughout Washington State.

The Mountaineers sponsors both classes and year-round outdoor activities in the Pacific Northwest, which include hiking, mountain climbing, ski-touring, snowshoeing, bicycling, camping, kayaking and canoeing, nature study, sailing, and adventure travel. The club's conservation division supports environmental causes through educational activities, sponsoring legislation, and presenting informational programs. All club activities are led by skilled, experienced volunteers, who are dedicated to promoting safe and responsible enjoyment and preservation of the outdoors.

If you would like to participate in these organized outdoor activities or the club's programs, consider a membership in The Mountaineers. For information and an application, write or call The Mountaineers, Club Headquarters, 300 Third Avenue West, Seattle, Washington 98119; (206) 284-6310.

The Mountaineers Books, an active, nonprofit publishing program of the club, produces guidebooks, instructional texts, historical works, natural history guides, and works on environmental conservation. All books produced by The Mountaineers are aimed at fulfilling the club's mission.

Send or call for our catalog of more than 300 outdoor titles:

The Mountaineers Books
1001 SW Klickitat Way, Suite 201
Seattle, WA 98134
1-800-553-4453
e-mail: mbooks@mountaineers.org

Other titles you may enjoy from The Mountaineers:

50 HIKES IN™ HELLS CANYON & OREGON'S WALLOWAS,
Rhonda & George Ostertag
A comprehensive guide to the well-traveled and unbeaten trails of Hells
Canyon and Oregon's Wallowas. Includes hikes for every level of expertise,
maps, local camping options, permit requirements, and tips on gear, safety,
and backcountry etiquette.

**THE WATERFALL LOVER'S GUIDE TO THE PACIFIC NORTH-
WEST, 2nd Ed.: Where to Find More Than 500 Scenic Waterfalls in
Washington, Oregon & Idaho,** *Gregory A. Plumb*
A five-star system rates waterfalls accessible to dayhikers and Sunday drivers.

**EXPLORING OREGON'S WILD AREAS, 2nd Ed.: A Guide for
Hikers, Backpackers, Climbers, X-C Skiers, & Paddlers,** *William Sullivan*
A complete resource covering 65 of the state's lesser-known and unbeaten
beautiful places, including wilderness areas, wildlife refuges, nature preserves,
and state parks.

**MAC'S FIELD GUIDES: Northwest Park/Backyard Birds, Northwest
Trees, Pacific Northwest Wildflowers,** *Craig MacGowan & David Sauskojus*
Two-sided plastic laminated cards, developed by a teacher of marine science,
with color drawings, common and scientific names, and information on size
and habitat.

ANIMAL TRACKS: PACIFIC NORTHWEST, Book & Poster,
Chris Stall
Both book and poster offer information on 40-50 animals common to the
Pacific Northwest region.

HIKING OREGON'S GEOLOGY, *Ellen Bishop & John Allen*
A guide to Oregon's most scenic and geologically interesting places, featuring
information to help you understand the state's geologic history. Hikes range
from strolls in urban parks to wilderness summit clubs.

100 HIKES IN™ OREGON, *Rhonda & George Ostertag*
Part of the series of fully detailed, best-selling hiking guides.